TIM. FOR POETRY

A WORKSHOP APPROACH FOR CXC

compiled by

Nahdjla Carasco Bailey

Nelson Caribbean

Thomas Nelson and Sons Ltd
Nelson House   Mayfield Road
Walton-on-Thames   Surrey
KT12 5PL   UK

51 York Place
Edinburgh
EH1 3JD   UK

Thomas Nelson (Hong Kong) Ltd
Toppan Building 10/F
22A Westlands Road
Quarry Bay   Hong Kong

Thomas Nelson Australia
102 Dodds Street
South Melbourne
Victoria 3205   Australia

Nelson Canada
1120 Birchmount Road
Scarborough   Ontario
M1K 5G4   Canada

© Nahdjla Carasco Bailey 1988

First published by Thomas Nelson and Sons Ltd 1988

ISBN 0-17-566351-3

NPN 10 9 8 7 6 5

Printed in Hong Kong

CONTENTS

To the Teacher

To the Reader

Part One

Dawn is a fisherman, his
harpoon of light*
Raymond Barrow   2

In all my wanderings round
this world of care
Oliver Goldsmith   4

'Tis said they are a grasping lot
Frank Collymore   6

Her face like a rain-beaten
stone when she rolled off
Theodore Roethke   8

The glories of our blood and
state
James Shirley   10

The grey sea and the long black
land
Robert Browning   12

Underneath the abject willow
W.H. Auden   14

Having measured the years
today by the calendar
Derek Walcott   16

Laughter with us is no great
undertaking
Martin Armstrong   18

Africa my Africa
David Diop   20

Like rain it sounded, till it
curved
Emily Dickinson   22

Your mouth contorting with
brief spite
Mervyn Morris   24

Horatio, of ideal courage vain
Mary Lamb   26

And there is an anger
Edwin Thumboo   28

By sundown we came to a
hidden village
Henry Treece   30

Earth has not anything to show
more fair
William Wordsworth   32

Turn sideways now and let
them see
H.A. Vaughan   34

Long had I thought
Una Marson   36

Part Two

Jamaican Fisherman
Sir Philip Sherlock   40

Academic
James Reeves   41

A Solution
Ogden Nash   42

Flowers
Dennis Craig   43

Sonnet
William Shakespeare   44

The Lesson
Edward Lucie-Smith   45

Lunch Hour
Judy Miles   46

Bird
Dennis Scott   48

Road to Lacovia
A.L. Hendriks   50

In the Gentle Afternoon
Royston Ellis   51

* The poems in Part 1 are listed under their first lines, not by title. See note on
p. viii.

Canes by the Roadside
A.N. Forde   52

The Muse's Complaint
Kendel Hippolyte   54

The Fox and the Cat
James Vincent Cunningham   56

The Send-off
Wilfred Owen   58

If I have Sinned in Act
Hartley Coleridge   59

Ancestor on the Auction Block
Vera Bell   60

A Wheel called Progress
Cecil Gray   62

Hawk Roosting
Ted Hughes   64

Before the Scales, Tomorrow
Otto René Castillo   65

Light Love
Roger Mais   66

Flame-heart
Claude McKay   68

'Twas Ever Thus
H.S. Leigh   70

The Riders
Barnabas J. Ramon-Fortuné   71

Ulysses (extract)
Alfred, Lord Tennyson   72

Part Three

Carrion Crows
A.J. Seymour   76

A Small Tragedy
Sally Roberts   77

History Makers
George Campbell   78

Music a Kind of Sleep
Basil McFarlane   79

Song of Myself (extract)
Walt Whitman   80

Looking at your Hands
Martin Carter   82

Character of a Happy Life
Sir Henry Wotton   83

The Best of School
D.H. Lawrence   84

Choice
Gordon Allen North   86

Anancy
Andrew Salkey   87

In our Land
Harold M. Telemaque   88

Ave Maria
Barbara Ferland   89

In Memoriam
Alfred Pragnell   90

The Tide
Bevinda Noronha   91

The Maroon Girl
Walter Adolphe Roberts   92

Isabella (extract)
John Keats   93

The Listeners
Walter de la Mare   94

Do not Go Gentle into that
Good Night
Dylan Thomas   96

The Pawpaw
Edward Kamau Brathwaite   97

Behind Shutters
Merle Collins   98

Beggarman
Errol Hill   100

Shoppin' Trips
Susan Wallace   102

On a Spaniel called Beau
Killing a Young Bird
William Cowper   103

Moments
John Robert Lee   104

The Microbe
Hilaire Belloc   105

A Carol in Minor
E. McG. Keane   106

The Torchbearers (extract)
Alfred Noyes   108

Spring Feast
John Figueroa   109

Pygmalion and Galatea
H.D. Carberry   110

I Shall Go Back
Wilmot Sanowar   111

Tempus
N.R. Carasco Bailey   112

Glossary   *113*

Index of Poets and Poems   *115*

v

ACKNOWLEDGEMENTS

For the inspiration that their kind gestures afforded me: special thanks to each of the many students who made a point of personally conveying to me their pleasure and satisfaction with the new-found benefits they had derived from being exposed consistently to the kinds of poetry exercises now presented in this book. Thanks also to the two faculty members who themselves took time to relay to me the positive comments they had heard from my students concerning their classroom experiences with poetry (through the means presented in this text). Thanks to Janet Forde, Robert Lee and the staff of the Sir Arthur Lewis Community College Library for making material easily accessible. Special thanks to Leonie St Juste, lecturer in Language Arts, for the loan of several resource books, and to the teachers who shared with me their experiences of poetry teaching in the classroom, both negative and positive; to Agatha of International Business Services for unhesitatingly accepting the job of typing the material; to Freya Watkinson of Thomas Nelson and Sons for her belief in the collection, and for her valuable guidance; to Alice McIlroy for her ready and worthwhile assistance.

NRCB

Nahdjla Carasco Bailey and the publishers are grateful to the following for permission to use copyright material in this book: Cape Goliard Press and Otto René Castillo for 'Before the Scales, Tomorrow' from *Let's Go!* translated by Margaret Randall; Dennis R. Craig for 'Flowers'; 'A Solution' reproduced by permission of Curtis Brown Ltd, on behalf of the estate of Ogden Nash; Faber and Faber Ltd, for 'Elegy' from *Collected Poems of Theodore Roethke*, 'Conquerors' from *The Haunted Garden* by Henry Treece and 'Underneath the Abject Willow' from *Collected Poems* by W.H. Auden; 'Hawk Roosting' reprinted by permission of Faber and Faber Ltd from *Lupercal* by Ted Hughes; 'Elegy' from *In a Green Night* by Derek Walcott. Copyright © 1962 by Derek Walcott. Reprinted by permission of Farrar, Straus and Giroux, Inc.; John Figueroa for 'Spring Feast'; Cecil Gray for 'A Wheel Called Progress'; A.L. Hendriks for 'Road to Lacovia'; David Higham Associates Ltd., for 'Do not go gentle into that good night' from *Poems* by Dylan Thomas, published by J.M. Dent and Sons Ltd.; Errol Hill for 'Beggarman'; Kendel Hyppolyte for 'The Muse's Complaint'; J.R. Lee for 'Moments'; The Literary Trustees of Walter de la Mare and the Society of Authors as their

TO THE TEACHER

You will see at once that this is not just another anthology. As a teacher myself, I have had not only the student but you also, very much in mind in the careful planning of this material. The material is arranged to aid you in your teaching, whether you are giving your students independent class work to do or whether the work is more teacher-directed, whether you are engaging them in group work with student-to-student exchanges or whether you are setting homework. *You* decide when to use the various sections and for what purposes. What is certain is that you will find ample opportunity for valuable involvement of the students with these poems, by way of the variety of questions and activities offered, and by exploration of the underlying theme of 'time' running throughout the book.

A special note on Part 3 with its creative exercises: do not underestimate these; take time to fit them into your programme. They afford the student a further, sounder relationship with poetry through means and methods which, unfortunately, are not normally given time in the classroom. Also, encourage as much as is practical the sharing of these creative efforts by students.

Generally, students are fascinated by poetry for what it is, and take pride in becoming more and more comfortable with it. I believe that the objective testing of poetry, through its method of dissection and discrimination, has a major role to play for the vast majority of students in leading them towards demystification of and independence in dealing with the language of poetry. They benefit from the definite transfer value which results from regular practice of this.

Before you begin to use the poems with students, make sure that they have a good understanding of the kind of information listed on page x. Have a general discussion on these items with your class. Stress the importance of the intelligent reading of poetry, the simple truth being that much poetry that is misunderstood is that which is ill-read (by students themselves or others).

Finally, I can say from experience that if you expose your students regularly to the various types of exercises in this book, you will find that, besides their obvious greater ease with and understanding of poetry itself, they will develop positive spill-over effects into a better handling of prose, whether comprehending it, analysing it or creating it. Give this method a try. It works.

Note The poems in Part 1 are untitled so as not to give away their subject matter and so make the student's task less of a thinking one than it ought to be.

NRCB

TO THE READER

Read each poem aloud intelligently and with expression. Pay attention to punctuation, pauses, run-on lines, rhythm, rhyme, tone and mood. You should be able to read it better the second time and even better the third. Read each poem as many times as you need to for understanding, interpretation and appreciation.

Remember to ask yourself questions as you reread the poems. Think about who is speaking and to whom, and the type of people they are. Look at the setting (time, place and occasion). Consider the main purpose behind the poem, the poet's intention in writing it, and the main idea conveyed. A good way of doing this is to write a short but full restatement of the poem in ordinary prose answering the question 'Who is doing what, where and when, and how and why has the poet expressed this?'

Find again the parts which you need to take a closer look at for understanding. Try to absorb the general 'feel' of the poem.

Subject

Now ask yourself what the poem is about at a concrete level. That is, for example, what exactly is happening in the poem? What or who is being described? What is being done, said, talked about, argued, expressed, worked out? Who is talking (the 'I' of the poem) to whom? About what? When and where? (e.g., setting).

Tone

See if you can get a sense of how the poet feels about his or her subject matter (i.e. the poet's attitude to it) and therefore how he or she puts over that feeling to you − in what tone (of voice) the poet is speaking and writing.

Consider whether the tone is serious, concerned, chatty, casual, ironic, exaggerated, critical, happy, sad, sincere, sarcastic, amused, sympathetic, aggressive, lighthearted, bold, disrespectful, dictatorial, and so on. There will be many others that will occur to you. Think well about a suitable word for the tone that you detect. Remember, too, that the poet may be using more than one tone − a combination of tones − to get the meaning across to you.

Mood

You will also sense there is a mood to each poem, that is, the effect which is created by the poem, the atmosphere which surrounds the poem. Consider whether this mood is serious, heavy, joyful, bitter, thoughtful, reflective, quiet, sad, calm, angry, peaceful and so on.

Theme

Then look to see what the poem all adds up to, what it means, what the main or overall idea behind it is, what the message being communicated is. The answer will provide you with the main theme of the poem.

The poet's purpose

Next ask yourself why you think the poet wrote the poem. What was the reason, purpose, intention, aim? Was it a desire to describe or depict a person, place, thing or idea? To express and share a particular feeling or experience with you, the reader? To relate a story in a certain way, to make a point, to persuade you, to arouse a particular feeling in you, to offer an opinion, to protest an idea, to amuse and entertain, to reflect on, examine, or consider an idea or condition? To honour or praise someone or something?

Other intentions will occur to you as you read the poems. Consider not only the actual subject matter and theme of the poem but also the tone in which they are treated and the general mood that is evident. You will also need to look at how the poem is constructed.

Technical construction

To do this you will need to consider the techniques the poet has used to create, reinforce and project the meaning, effect and intention of the poem. This is important not just as an exercise in spotting poetic devices, but for seeing exactly how the devices used work hand in hand with the ideas being put across and the mood being created.

Some technical points to consider are:
   the type of poem, and its setting;
   the structure of the poem;
   the rhythm (i.e. the beat, the flow of the words);
   the choice of language used (whether simple, complex,
      standard English, dialect, figurative, suggestive,
      precise, symbolic and so on;
   the shape and form (where significant);
   the rhyme (end rhyme and internal rhyme);
   the punctuation;
   stylistic devices such as contrast, illustration, repetition,
      imagery, antithesis, litotes, symbolism, irony,
      paradox, rhetorical questioning, climax, hyperbole,
      simile, oxymoron, metaphor, personification,
      alliteration, onomatopoeia.

Understanding and appreciation

All aspects of the poem are related, so although we analyse the poem in parts, these parts must always be put back together to gain an overall understanding and appreciation of a poem.

Sometimes a poem may be deceptive. Its actual meaning may be very different from its apparent meaning. The poet may have used symbolism to represent a much larger idea or condition, and you may need to look for a deeper meaning at another level to really understand the poem.

As well as answering and discussing the questions accompanying each poem, try to keep these guidelines in mind, going back over the early poems again if necessary, analysing them in this way once you have gained experience.

Inside a Poem

It doesn't always have to rhyme,
but there's the repeat of a beat, somewhere
an inner chime that makes you want to
tap your feet or swerve in a curve;
a lilt, a leap, lightning-split: —
thunderstruck the consonants jut,
while the vowels open wide as waves in the noon-blue sea.

You hear with your heels, your eyes feel
what they never touched before:
fins on a bird, feathers on a deer;
taste all colors, inhale
memory and tomorrow and always the tang is today.

EVE MERRIAM

NRCB
June 1987

To Eliot, dark-haired...

PART ONE

Read each poem aloud intelligently and with expression.
Pay attention to punctuation, pauses, run-on lines,
rhythm, rhyme, tone and mood. Ask yourself
the questions *who*, *what*, *where*, *when*, *why* and *how*. You
should be able to read it better the second time and even
better the third. Read each poem as many times as
you need to for understanding, interpretation and
appreciation, and then attempt the questions following
each poem. Look again at the note to the reader on p. ix if
you need further help.

Dawn is a fisherman, his harpoon of light
Poised for a throw — so swiftly morning comes:
The darkness squats upon the sleeping land
Like a flung cast-net, and the black shapes of boats
5   Lie hunched like nesting turtles
On the flat calm of the sea.

Among the trees the houses peep at the stars
Blinking farewell, and half-awakened birds
Hurtle across the vista, some in the distance
10   Giving their voice self-criticized auditions.

Warning comes from the cocks, their necks distended
Like city trumpeters: and suddenly
Between the straggling fences of grey cloud
The sun, a barefoot boy, strides briskly up
15   The curved beach of the sky, flinging his greetings
Warmly in all directions, laughingly saying
Up, up, the day is here! Another day is here!

RAYMOND BARROW

1 The subject matter of the poem is concerned with
    (A) the silence of the night.
    (B) the various sounds of twilight.
    (C) the advent of daybreak.
    (D) a fisherman making a catch.

2 What literary device does the poet use in lines 14 to 16?
    (A) extended metaphor
    (B) understatement (litotes)
    (C) extended personification
    (D) anticlimax

3 Why do 'the stars blink farewell'?
    (A) Because they become covered by thick, grey cloud.
    (B) To say goodnight to people just going to bed.
    (C) To attract the sleepy birds' attention.
    (D) Because in the imminent light, they will become invisible.

4 'Vista' (line 9) means
    (A) trees.
    (B) rooftops.
    (C) view.
    (D) grass.

5 Which phrase suggests to us that the birds appear to be competing with each other in song?
   (A) 'self-criticized auditions'   (C) 'half-awakened birds'
   (B) 'hurtle across the vista'   (D) 'giving their voice'

6 The noun which completes the simile '. . .like a flung cast-net' is
   (A) the land.   (C) the darkness.
   (B) the sea.   (D) the boats.

7 The purpose of the cocks' warning is
   (A) to drown the birds'   (C) to herald yet another
       singing.   sunrise.
   (B) to announce a grey day to (D) to imitate the sounds of
       the people.   the trumpeters.

8 The aspects of 'a barefoot boy' suggested in its context (line 14) are
   (A) poverty and loneliness.   (C) sadness and envy.
   (B) freedom and gaiety.   (D) inhibition and
                                     inexperience.

9 The poem is mainly
   (A) descriptive.   (C) narrative.
   (B) humorous.   (D) romantic.

10 The picture conveyed by the use of the word 'fences' (line 13) is that of
   (A) a solid and unbroken   (C) a vulnerable barrier.
       obstacle.   (D) a necessary inconvenience.
   (B) a purely decorative
       structure.

11 The basic technique which the poet employs for effect in the poem is
   (A) the clever use of rhyme.   (C) the generous use of
   (B) the strong appeal made to   contrast.
       our emotions.   (D) the use of closely
                                      associated images side by
                                      side.

12 In one sentence say what the poet's intention is in this poem.

13 There is a contrast in mood between the early part of the poem and the ending. What is the dominant mood of each part? How does the poet convey each mood?

14 What feelings are aroused in you by this poem?

15 Is your experience of the subject matter of the poem similar to or different from that of the poet?

In all my wanderings round this world of care,
In all my griefs — and God has given my share —
I still had hopes, my latest hours to crown,
Amidst these humble bowers to lay me down;
5   To husband out life's taper at the close,
And keep the flame from wasting by repose:
I still had hopes, for pride attends us still,
Amidst the swains to show my book-learned skill,
Around my fire an evening group to draw,
10 And tell of all I felt, and all I saw;
And, as a hare whom hounds and horn pursue
Pants to the place from whence at first she flew,
I still had hopes, my long vexations past,
Here to return — and die at home at last.

                              OLIVER GOLDSMITH

1 Which line tells us that the poet's life had been an unhappy one?
   (A) line 11   (C) line 2
   (B) line 14   (D) line 1

2 In his old age the poet hoped to
   (A) get married.   (C) get an education.
   (B) return home.   (D) die quickly.

3 This poetry is
   (A) impersonal.
   (B) humorous.
   (C) reflective.
   (D) narrative.

4 The prevailing mood of the poem is one of
   (A) despondency.
   (B) indifference.
   (C) optimism.
   (D) pessimism.

5 The word 'taper' means
   (A) span.
   (B) candle.
   (C) yardstick.
   (D) worry.

6 The poet intended to satisfy his pride by
   (A) sitting next to a cosy fire.
   (B) going out hunting.
   (C) becoming someone's husband.
   (D) displaying his acquired knowledge.

7 Which two lines suggest that the poet had been forced to leave his native home?
   (A) lines 1 and 2
   (B) lines 11 and 12
   (C) lines 9 and 10
   (D) lines 8 and 9

8 Line 5 tells us that the poet hoped to
   (A) take his own life.
   (B) find a wife when he returned home.
   (C) go wandering again.
   (D) lengthen and conserve his last days.

9 Where is it revealed that the poet had come to terms with former trials?
   (A) line 2
   (B) line 13
   (C) line 7
   (D) line 11

10 Which of the following words is NOT used figuratively?
   (A) swains (line 8)
   (B) flame (line 6)
   (C) crown (line 3)
   (D) taper (line 5)

11 The echo (line 14) of the hope expressed in line 4 has the effect of helping to
   (A) create a mood of impatience.
   (B) make the poem boring.
   (C) give unity to the poem.
   (D) make the poem morbid.

12 What do you think the poet's purpose is in this poem?

13 How would you describe the poet's feeling for his roots?

14 State some of the ideas which the poet is trying to communicate by means of the characteristics of the 'I' of the poem.

15 Can you identify with the poet's feelings and wishes?

'Tis said they are a grasping lot
   who grudge the peasant all;
Who chiefly live to fill their guts,
   And upon whom the call
Of all the finer things of life
   Is never known to fall;

Who only think and talk about
   Foreign manure and rains
And all the other things that serve
   To feed their greedy canes;
Who every night squat themselves down
   To gloat upon their gains.

Perhaps they do. I do not know
   Much about sugar-kings;
But I salute with gratitude
   The loving care which wrings
Such beauty from the soil and o'er
   Our land its patchwork flings.

FRANK COLLYMORE

1 The word 'grasping' (line 1) means
   (A) strange.   (C) greedy.
   (B) impolite.   (D) dangerous.

2 In stanzas 1 and 2 the poet relates what
   (A) he knows first-hand.   (C) he hears people say.
   (B) the sugar kings have told   (D) he thinks is true.
       him.

3 In stanza 1 we are told that 'they' are supposedly
   (A) unrefined.   (C) generous.
   (B) cultured.   (D) boring.

4 In stanza 2 we learn that 'they' are reportedly
   (A) conscious of others' needs. (C) not at all self-seeking
   (B) on friendly terms with   (D) obsessed with all aspects
       foreigners only.   of their occupation.

5 Line 1 of stanza 3 tells us that the poet
   (A) has every desire to learn   (C) regards the sugar-kings
       more about the peasants.   with great suspicion.
   (B) is unperturbed by what   (D) hopes to get better
       stanzas 1 and 2 tell us.   acquainted with the
                                       situation.

6 The poet begins to reveal his personal viewpoint to us in
   (A) line 12.   (C) line 15.
   (B) line 13.   (D) line 17.

7 The 'they' of the poem are
   (A) plantation owners.   (C) peasant farmers.
   (B) city bankers.   (D) foreign kings.

8 Which word refers to the patterned arrangement of units?
   (A) gains   (C) squat
   (B) sugar-kings   (D) patchwork

9 The poet ends by
   (A) criticising the dedication (C) opposing the sugar-kings
       of the planters.   and their work.
   (B) paying homage to the   (D) being negative about the
       planters.   products.

10 The main intention of the poet is
   (A) to describe the appearance (C) to offer an opinion on a
       of something.   situation.
   (B) to tell a story.   (D) to try to persuade the
                                       readers that he is right.

11 What, specifically, is this poem chiefly meant to communicate?

12 Pick out some obvious themes in this poem.

13 Do you share the poet's view of his subject? Expand.

7

Her face like a rain-beaten stone on the day she rolled off
With the dark hearse, and enough flowers for an alderman —
And so she was, in her way, Aunt Tilly.

Sighs, sighs, who says they have sequence?
5 Between the spirit and the flesh — what war?
She never knew:
For she asked no quarter and gave none,
Who sat with the dead when the relatives left,
Who fed and tended the infirm, the mad, the epileptic,
10 And, with a harsh rasp of a laugh at herself,
Faced up to the worst.

I recall how she harried the children away all the late summer
From the one beautiful thing in her yard, the peach tree;
How she kept the wizened, the fallen, the misshapen for herself,
15 And picked and pickled the best, to be left on rickety doorsteps.

And yet she died in agony,
Her tongue, at the last, thick, black as an ox's.

Terror of cops, bill collectors, betrayers of the poor —
I see you in some celestial supermarket
20 Moving serenely among the leeks and cabbages,
Probing the squash,
Bearing down, with two steady eyes,
On the quaking butcher.

THEODORE ROETHKE

8

1 The feature of Aunt Tilly which the poet emphasises most is
   (A) her sorrow.   (C) her selflessness.
   (B) her humour.   (D) her fearsomeness.

2 The word 'alderman' (line 2) means
   (A) bride.   (C) high-ranking city official.
   (B) wreath.   (D) old woman.

3 'And so she was, in her way' (line 3) refers to the words
   (A) 'an alderman'.   (C) 'dark hearse'.
   (B) 'Aunt Tilly'.   (D) 'enough flowers'.

4 Which one of the following devices does the poet NOT use?
   (A) simile   (C) onomatopoeia
   (B) rhetorical question   (D) paradox

5 In their contexts, 'Terror' (line 18) and 'quaking' (line 23) bear
   testimony to Aunt Tilly's
   (A) weakness in the eyes of a   (C) absolute wickedness.
   few.   (D) hateful nature.
   (B) fearsomeness to some.

6 Lines 14 and 15 attest to Aunt Tilly's
   (A) cooking ability.   (C) mean nature and selfish
   (B) generosity and concern for   heart.
   the underprivileged.   (D) love of agriculture.

7 The poet's attitude to the subject of the poem is best described as
   one of
   (A) great admiration.   (C) mild dislike.
   (B) total indifference.   (D) utter disappointment.

8 The word 'celestial' expresses the poet's feeling that Aunt Tilly is
   (A) in purgatory.   (C) in heaven.
   (B) in a grocery shop.   (D) in hell.

9 An example of alliteration is to be found in
   (A) line 9.   (C) line 22.
   (B) line 4.   (D) line 8.

10 Illustrations are given of Aunt Tilly's
   (A) determination and   (C) obedience and knowledge.
   resilience.   (D) forgetfulness and naïvety.
   (B) fearfulness and hesitancy.

11 In what tone or tones is this poem written?

12 Why do you think the poet wrote this poem?

13 What shift comes in line 19 and what effect does it have,
   especially at the end of the poem?

14 Justify the poet's vision of Aunt Tilly as expressed in lines 19 to
   23, by reference to earlier parts of the poem.

The glories of our blood and state
　　Are shadows, not substantial things;
There is no armour against fate;
　　Death lays his icy hand on kings:
5　　　　Sceptre and crown,
　　　　Must tumble down,
And in the dust be equal made
With the poor crooked scythe and spade.

Some men with swords may reap the field,
10　　And plant fresh laurels where they kill:
But their strong nerves at last must yield;
　　They tame but one another still;
　　　　Early or late
　　　　They stoop to fate,
15 And must give up their murmuring breath
When they, pale captives, creep to death.

The garlands wither on your brow;
　　Then boast no more your mighty deeds;
Upon Death's purple altar now
20　　See where the victor-victim bleeds:
　　　　Your heads must come
　　　　To the cold tomb;
Only the actions of the just
Smell sweet, and blossom in their dust.

JAMES SHIRLEY

1　This poem has a very important message for us all, and may be
　summarised best by one of the following:
　(A) Good things come to those　(C) Death, where is thy sting?
　　　who wait.　　　　　　　　　(D) Death is a wonderful
　(B) Fate and Death are　　　　　　　release from a strife-torn
　　　inevitable and not　　　　　　　world.
　　　discriminating.

2 Which would NOT be a suitable title for the poem?
   (A) Death, the great leveller.
   (B) Remember, man, that thou art dust, and unto dust thou shalt return.
   (C) All men are born great.
   (D) Death is no respecter of persons.

3 'The evil that men do lives after them; the good is often interred with their bones.' Which two lines contradict this famous quotation?
   (A) lines 7 and 8
   (B) lines 15 and 16
   (C) lines 23 and 24
   (D) lines 19 and 20

4 Line 4 is an example of
   (A) onomatopoeia.
   (B) simile.
   (C) personification.
   (D) antithesis.

5 What, according to the poet, is the sole survivor when all is said and done?
   (A) 'The glories of our blood and state' (line 1)
   (B) 'Their strong nerves' (line 11)
   (C) 'The actions of the just' (line 23)
   (D) 'The garlands...on your brow' (line 17)

6 Which word below is not used literally in the poem?
   (A) purple (line 19)
   (B) deeds (line 18)
   (C) tomb (line 4)
   (D) just (line 23)

7 Which figure of speech is used in lines 5 to 8?
   (A) onomatopoeia
   (B) simile
   (C) antithesis
   (D) personification

8 The poet wrote this poem to make us feel
   (A) humble.
   (B) jealous.
   (C) proud.
   (D) happy.

9 A sudden change in the theme occurs in
   (A) line 23.
   (B) line 17.
   (C) line 20.
   (D) line 13.

10 In which of the following is the idea of contrast NOT contained?
   (A) line 2
   (B) lines 5 and 6
   (C) line 20
   (D) line 22

11 Identify two poetic devices used by the poet and say how each contributes to the poem's meaning.

12 Do you sympathize with the poet's assessment of his subject matter?

13 Look back at the poem about Aunt Tilly. Can you find any ideas in this poem by James Shirley that may have application for the former?

The grey sea and the long black land;
And the yellow half-moon large and low;
And the startled little waves that leap
In fiery ringlets from their sleep,
5　　As I gain the cove with pushing prow,
And quench its speed i' the slushy sand.

Then a mile of warm sea-scented beach;
Three fields to cross till a farm appears;
A tap at the pane, the quick sharp scratch
10　　And blue spurt of a lighted match,
And a voice less loud, thro' its joys and fears,
Than the two hearts beating each to each!

ROBERT BROWNING

1 The poet is
　(A) out for a late swim.
　(B) on his way to a house.
　(C) out for a moonlight stroll.
　(D) on a journey with no
　　　particular purpose.

2 In stanza 1 the poet travels
　(A) on foot.
　(B) by boat.
　(C) by car.
　(D) by none of the above.

3 Which of the following words is used metaphorically?
    (A) startled (line 3)   (C) slushy (line 6)
    (B) leap (line 3)   (D) tap (line 9)

4 The word 'cove' (line 5) means
    (A) big cave.   (C) small bay.
    (B) wide beach.   (D) tall tree.

5 The poet employs all of the following devices EXCEPT
    (A) alliteration.   (C) simile.
    (B) climax.   (D) metaphor.

6 The word 'its' (line 6) refers to
    (A) prow.   (C) speed.
    (B) cove.   (D) sand.

7 The pervading mood in the poem is one of
    (A) wonder.   (C) restlessness.
    (B) expectation.   (D) indifference.

8 The 'quick sharp scratch' (line 9) is a direct reaction to
    (A) the lighting of a match.   (C) the tap at the pane.
    (B) the joyful voice.   (D) the beating hearts.

9 In order to highlight the depth of feeling experienced by the person in the poem, the poet
    (A) paints a vivid picture of   (C) introduces the idea of
        nature.   light.
    (B) talks of the sudden action (D) contrasts two particular
        of the waves.   sounds.

10 The main event of the poem is
    (A) the disturbing of the   (C) the arrival of the poet at
        waves.   the beach.
    (B) the meeting of loved ones. (D) the rising of the moon.

11 The reader is left with the impression that the poet
    (A) is unsure of the way.   (C) is unenthusiastic about the
    (B) has been this way before.   journey.
                              (D) is taking this route for the
                              first time.

12 At what point in the build-up to the main event does the rhythm show an obvious increase in pace and intensity? What is the effect of this acceleration, and how does the punctuation, at this point, contribute to the effect?

13 What main theme underlies this poem?

14 How does the poem make you feel?

15 Pick out some images from the poem and show how each contributes to the mood at that point in the poem.

Underneath the abject willow,
    Lover, sulk no more:
Act from thought should quickly follow.
    What is thinking for?
5   Your unique and moping station
        Proves you cold;
        Stand up and fold
Your map of desolation.

Bells that toll across the meadows
10   From the sombre spire
Toll for these unloving shadows
    Love does not require.
All that lives may love; why longer
        Bow to loss
15   With arms across?
Strike and you shall conquer.

Geese in flocks above you flying
    Their direction know,
Brooks beneath the thin ice flowing
20   To their oceans go.
Dark and dull is your distraction,
        Walk then, come,
        No longer numb
Into your satisfaction.

                W.H. AUDEN

---

1 In the first stanza the theme can be summed up as follows:
  (A) You're feeling cold out
      there, so come inside.
  (B) Rise and fold up the chart
      you're reading.
  (C) Don't just sit there
      moping, do something
      positive.
  (D) Think a little more before
      you act.

2 The situation in the poem surrounds
   (A) a girl waiting to meet a   (C) a little shepherd boy.
       suitor.   (D) a soldier about to go to
   (B) a forlorn lover.   battle.

3 The mood of the person being addressed in the poem is best
  described as one of
   (A) exuberance.   (C) grief and despair.
   (B) hatred and fear.   (D) confidence and optimism.

4 Which two words are NOT used literally in the poem?
   (A) sulk and spire (lines 2 and   (C) geese and brooks (lines 17
       10)   and 19)
   (B) map and strike (lines 8   (D) meadows and distraction
       and 16)   (lines 9 and 21)

5 In the second stanza the person spoken to is told to
   (A) go off to war and win.   (C) be patient and wait for
   (B) take revenge on those who   love.
       hurt him.   (D) take a bold step and find
                                         love again.

6 Which lines portray the idea that all things have a sense of
  purpose?
   (A) lines 5 to 8   (C) lines 21 to 24
   (B) lines 9 to 12   (D) lines 17 to 20

7 The poet is confident that if his friend follows the advice given
  throughout, he
   (A) will be in a worse state   (C) will acquire material
       than before.   wealth.
   (B) will prosper spiritually and (D) will achieve happiness and
       morally.   contentment.

8 Which of the following phrases most accurately describes the tone
  of the poem?
   (A) sarcastic rejection   (C) friendly concern
   (B) humourous affection   (D) good-natured tolerance

9 Show how the central idea of the poem (the main theme) is
  reinforced through somewhat varied appeals, but all to the same
  end.

10 Do you like this poem or not? Why or why not?

11 What reasons can you give for not supposing that the poet is
   himself the object of the 'you' of the poem's distress?

Having measured the years today by the calendar
That marks your seventeenth death, I stayed until
It was the honest hour to remember
How this house has lived with and without you well.
5 And I do not chide death's hand,
Nor can I hurl death taunts or tantrums
Because the washing faiths my father walked are no more light,
And all the gulls that were tall as his dreams
Are one with his light rotting in this sand.

10 I shall not hurl death taunts or tantrums,
Nor blast with violent words the yellow grave
Under the crooked tree, where Lazarus lies like history,
For greater than death is death's gift, that can,
Behind the bright dust that was the skeleton,

15 (Who drank the wine and believed the blessed bread)
Can make us see the forgotten price of man
Shine from the perverse beauty of the dead.

DEREK WALCOTT

1 The phrase 'seventeenth death' indicates that
(A) the poet's father died at
the age of seventeen.
(B) it is the seventeenth
anniversary of the poet's
father's death.
(C) the poet's father died on
the seventeenth day of the
month.
(D) the poet was seventeen
when his father died.

2 His father's is a 'yellow grave' (line 11) because
(A) it is covered with yellow
blossoms.
(B) it holds the body of a
coward.
(C) it is sandy, parched and
old.
(D) the sun is shining brightly
on it.

16

3 The poet
(A) fears death's sting.
(B) longs for death's release.
(C) hates death for its cruelty.
(D) sees some virtue in death.

4 He looks at death in this way (as in question 3) because he feels that
(A) death is so unpredictable.
(B) people are relieved of this cruel world through death.
(C) the memory of a person's real worth is enhanced after death.
(D) death leaves only despair behind.

5 The explanation (in 4 above) is to be found in
(A) lines 10 and 11.
(B) lines 3 and 4.
(C) lines 6 and 7.
(D) lines 16 and 17.

6 The bracketed line in the poem is spoken of
(A) the skeleton.
(B) the poet.
(C) the poet's father.
(D) none of the above.

7 That same line tells us that
(A) the poet's father was a priest.
(B) the poet is a sinner.
(C) the poet eats and drinks heartily.
(D) the poet's father was a church-going man.

8 'Perverse' (line 17) means
(A) different from what is reasonably expected.
(B) for a short time only.
(C) superior.
(D) genuine and sincere.

9 Personification is employed in
(A) line 10.
(B) line 16.
(C) line 12.
(D) line 5.

10 This poem most easily belongs in one of the following categories:
(A) narrative.
(B) love.
(C) reflective.
(D) descriptive.

11 What is the poet's purpose in writing this poem?

12 How would you describe the tone in which the poet is writing?

13 The poem expresses certain ideas prompted by an occasion. State the main ideas which the poet is trying to communicate.

14 In lines 13 to 17 Walcott is stating a view that has already been aired (albeit less deliberately) in one of the earlier poems in Part 1 of this book. Do you recognise the other poem and recall the way the other poet put forward his (related) view?

Laughter with us is no great undertaking;
A sudden wave that breaks and dies in breaking.
Laughter, with Mrs Reece, is much less simple:
It germinates, it spreads, dimple by dimple,
From small beginnings, things of easy girth,
To formidable redundancies of mirth.
Clusters of subterranean chuckles rise,
And presently the circles of her eyes
Close into slits, and all the woman heaves.
As a great elm with all its mounds of leaves
Wallows before the storm. From hidden sources
A mustering of blind volcanic forces
Takes her and shakes her till she sobs and gapes
Then all that load of bottled mirth escapes
In one wild crow, a lifting of huge hands
And creaking stays, a visage that expands
In scarlet ridge and furrow. Thence collapse,
A hanging head, a feeble hand that flaps
An apron-end to stir an air and waft
A steaming face. . . And Mrs Reece has laughed.

MARTIN ARMSTRONG

1 According to the poet, laughter with us is
  (A) short-lived.   (C) boring.
  (B) long lasting.   (D) sad.

2 Line 3 tells us that Mrs Reece's laughter is
  (A) more or less the same as (C) a far more complicated
      ours.   affair than ours.
  (B) much simpler than ours. (D) not as great an experience
                                as ours.

3 The period of Mrs Reece's laughing is traced by the poet through
the use of
(A) puns.   (C) alliteration.
(B) similes.   (D) climax.

4 The word 'subterranean' (line 7) tells us that Mrs Reece's
chuckles
(A) were high-pitched.   (C) did not last very long.
(B) came from deep down   (D) were louder than usual.
    inside her.

5 The word 'visage' (line 16) means
(A) view.   (C) picture.
(B) face.   (D) field.

6 An example of the use of alliteration is
(A) line 1.   (C) line 12.
(B) line 20.   (D) line 18.

7 Onomatopoeia is made use of in which one of the following
phrases from the poem?
(A) 'volcanic forces'   (C) 'bottled mirth'
(B) 'hidden sources'   (D) 'creaking stays'

8 The turning point in the poem, representing the start of falling
action, commences with
(A) 'As' (line 10).   (C) 'Takes' (line 13).
(B) 'Thence' (line 17).   (D) 'From' (line 5).

9 Mrs Reece's 'huge hands' are now 'feeble hands' because
(A) by the end of the poem   (C) she is worn out from her
    she is old.   experience of laughing.
(B) She has lost some weight.   (D) they have been damaged
                                       in a volcanic eruption.

10 The poet is writing in which one of the following moods?
(A) satirical   (C) nostalgic
(B) lighthearted   (D) serious

11 Why do you think the poet wrote this poem?

12 This poem is replete with images – both literal and non-literal.
Identify some which you like best and say why you appreciate
them.

13 Can you detect the lines where the rhythm is broken up,
warming up, not yet flowing, and then the lines where it begins to
flow. Suggest reasons for the use of each kind of rhythm in the
poem.

Africa my Africa
Africa of proud warriors in ancestral savannahs
Africa of whom my grandmother sings
On the banks of the distant river
5 I have never known you
But your blood flows in my veins
Your beautiful black blood that irrigates the fields
The blood of your sweat
The sweat of your work
10 The work of your slavery
The slavery of your children
Africa tell me Africa
Is this you this back that is bent
This back that breaks under the weight of humiliation
15 This back trembling with red scars
And saying yes to the whip under the midday sun
But a grave voice answers me
Impetuous son that tree young and strong
That tree there
20 In splendid loneliness amidst white and faded flowers
That is Africa your Africa
That grows again patiently obstinately
And its fruit gradually acquire
The bitter taste of liberty.

DAVID DIOP

---

1 The poet is obviously
  (A) born and living in Africa.
  (B) of African descent but born abroad.
  (C) indifferent to the fate of Africa.
  (D) born abroad but living in Africa.

2 The poet's initial view of Africa is that of
  (A) a land of self-respect and toil.
  (B) a war-ridden country.
  (C) a country of shame and woe.
  (D) a land of leisure and song.

3 This view may have been influenced by
(A) his ignorance of African history.
(B) proud images such as those of his grandmother's songs.
(C) his direct experience of African life.
(D) his ancestors' tales of shame.

4 'Impetuous' (line 18) means
(A) intelligent.
(B) hypocritical.
(C) showing pity.
(D) lacking thought.

5 The poet sees Africa in a changed light starting at
(A) line 17.
(B) line 9.
(C) line 13.
(D) line 15.

6 This new light is one of
(A) pride and joy.
(B) acceptance and shame.
(C) greater glory than in earlier days.
(D) freedom and contentment.

7 The tree mentioned in line 19 is
(A) the symbol of a broken, faded Africa.
(B) a dying one with no future at all.
(C) the symbol of a liberated Africa.
(D) of little significance in the poem.

8 This tree shows the characteristic of
(A) defeat.
(B) infertility.
(C) resilience.
(D) pessimism.

9 The poet ends the poem on a note of
(A) diffidence.
(B) hopelessness.
(C) repentance.
(D) regeneration.

10 Which of the following words is used metaphorically?
(A) savannahs (line 2)
(B) banks (line 4)
(C) sun (line 16)
(D) back (line 13)

11 What is the effect of the particular style employed in the structure of lines 6 to 11?

12 Make up your own appropriate name for that kind of style. What label can you give to it?

13 What are some of the thoughts to be found in this poem, and how do they work towards the ultimate idea of liberty?

14 The poem is without punctuation. Does this have significance for the direction of its meaning?

15 Explain the use of 'bitter' in the last line.

Like rain it sounded, till it curved
And then I knew t'was wind;
It walked as wet as any wave
And swept as dry as sand.
5   When it had pushed itself away
To some remotest plain
A coming as of hosts was heard —
That was indeed the rain!
It filled the wells, it pleased the pools,
10 It warbled in the road,
It pulled the spigot from the hills
And let the floods abroad;
It loosened acres, lifted seas,
The sites of centres stirred,
15 Then like Elijah rode away
Upon a wheel of cloud.

EMILY DICKINSON

This poem by American poet Emily Dickinson is without a title.
However, it describes a cloudburst. It is full of precise and effective
images. Read it thoughtfully.

1 The poet uses the word 'indeed' (line 8) to
   (A) underline her certainty   (C) merely add to the rhythm
       now that the rain had   of the line.
       really come.   (D) indicate surprise at the
   (B) express surprise at the   rain's coming at that time.
       rain's coming at all.

2 An example of the use of antithesis may be found in
   (A) line 9.   (C) lines 3 and 4.
   (B) lines 11 and 12.   (D) line 1.

3 The word 'abroad' (line 12) means
   (A) over the sea.   (C) everywhere.
   (B) rush.   (D) in a foreign land.

4 Lines 9 to 15 impress us with
   (A) the power and majesty of   (C) the short duration of the
       the rain.   rainfall.
   (B) the total damage done by   (D) the lightness of the
       the rain.   rainfall.

5 The wind makes its exit in
   (A) lines 15 and 16.   (C) lines 1 and 2.
   (B) lines 3 and 4.   (D) lines 5 and 6.

6 Line 3 contains examples of
   (A) onomatopoeia and simile.   (C) simile and alliteration.
   (B) personification and   (D) alliteration and
       onomatopoeia.   onomatopoeia.

7 The image of Elijah puts us in mind of
   (A) gloom and doom.   (C) triumph and glory.
   (B) merriment and humour.   (D) silence and fear.

8 The word 'itself' (line 5) refers to
   (A) the plain.   (C) the sand.
   (B) the rain.   (D) the wind.

9 The most suitable of these four titles for the poem would be:
   (A) Before the rain   (C) The advent of rain
   (B) The wind   (D) After the rain

10 Which of the following combinations of senses is appealed to in
   the poem?
   (A) hearing and taste   (C) sight and taste
   (B) touch and smell   (D) hearing and sight

11 Look again at the numerous images which the poet employs.
   Which ones appeal to you most and why?

12 What is the poet's specific purpose in this poem?

13 Relate the characteristics and behaviour of the rain to those of
   Mrs Reece in the earlier poem. Look for similarities and
   contrasts.

Your mouth contorting in brief spite and
Hurt, your laughter metamorphosed into howls,
Your frame so recently relaxed now tight
With three-year-old frustration, your bright eyes
5   Swimming tears, splashing your bare feet,
You stand there angling for a moment's hint
Of guilt or sorrow for the quick slap struck.

The ogre towers above you, that grim giant,
Empty of feeling, a colossal cruel,
10   Soon victim of the tale's conclusion, dead
At last. You hate him, you imagine
Chopping clean the tree he's scrambling down
Or plotting deeper pits to trap him in.

You cannot understand, not yet,
15   The hurt your easy tears can scald him with,
Nor guess the wavering hidden behind that mask.
This fierce man longs to lift you, curb your sadness
With piggy-back or bull-fight, anything,
But dare not ruin the lessons you should learn.

20   You must not make a plaything of the rain.

MERVYN MORRIS

———————————

24

1 It is obvious that the person being addressed in this poem is
  (A) a parent.   (C) a child.
  (B) a stranger.   (D) a lover.

2 The word nearest in meaning to 'contorting' is
  (A) moving.   (C) smiling.
  (B) changing.   (D) twisting.

3 The poet makes use of contrast in
  (A) stanza 3 only.   (C) stanza 2 only.
  (B) stanzas 1 and 3.   (D) none of the above.

4 Examples of onomatopoeia can be found in
  (A) lines 13 and 15.   (C) lines 6 and 16.
  (B) lines 9 and 18.   (D) lines 2 and 5.

5 Line 16 brings out the idea of
  (A) conflicting emotions.   (C) total confusion.
  (B) rank hypocrisy.   (D) unfeeling response.

6 'This fierce man' (line 17) is most likely to be
  (A) a friend.   (C) a father.
  (B) a servant.   (D) a brother.

7 The 'you' of the poem attempts to ease his hurt by
  (A) killing the unfeeling giant. (C) fantasising a convenient
  (B) making friends with his   ending to the episode.
      'aggressor'.   (D) unmasking the fierce man.

8 '. . . tears can scald him with' (line 15) contains elements of
  (A) alliteration, simile and   (C) metaphor, hyperbole and
      personification.   irony.
  (B) onomatopoeia, antithesis (D) alliteration, onomatopoeia
      and paradox.   and simile.

9 'You stand there . . .' (line 6)
  (A) daring him to repeat his   (C) feeling very guilty for
      action.   what you've done.
  (B) hoping to catch one slight (D) thinking of giving him a
      glimpse of sympathy in   quick slap.
      him.

10 'This fierce man' dare not relent because
  (A) he is too hurt.   (C) he wouldn't know how to.
  (B) you have been   (D) your lesson must not be
      unbelievably bad.   sacrificed.

11 Explain the significance of the last line of the poem.

12 What is the effect created by it standing alone?

13 Do you think the poet features directly in the poem although he has not used 'I'? If you do, or don't, what gives you that feeling? Justify your answer.

Horatio, of ideal courage vain,
Was flourishing in air his father's cane,
And as the fumes of valour swell'd his pate,
Now thought himself this Hero, and now that:
5   'And now,' he cried, 'I will Achilles be;
My sword I brandish; see, the Trojans flee.
Now I'll be Hector, when his angry blade
A lane through heaps of slaughtered Grecians made!
And now by deeds still braver I'll evince,
10   I am no less than Edward the Black Prince.
Give way, ye coward French': as thus he spoke,
And aim'd in fancy a sufficient stroke
To fix the fate of Crecy or Poitiers;
(The muse relates the Hero's fate with tears)
15   He struck his milk-white hand against a nail,
Sees his own blood, and feels his courage fail.
Ah! where is now that boasted valour flown,
That in the tented field so late was shown!
Achilles weeps, Great Hector hangs his head,
20   And the Black Prince goes whimpering to bed.

MARY LAMB

1 The real name of the 'I' of the poem is
   (A) Hector.   (C) Horatio.
   (B) Achilles.   (D) Edward.

2 From the poem we learn that Hector confronted
   (A) the Greeks.   (C) the French.
   (B) the Trojans.   (D) none of the above.

3 In the eyes of our 'hero' which of the following performed the most courageous acts?
   (A) Hector   (C) Achilles
   (B) Horatio   (D) The Black Prince

4 Who is the 'I' of the poem likely to be?
   (A) a soldier   (C) a mature man
   (B) a young boy   (D) a real hero

5 'Courage' turns to fear when
   (A) Horatio sees his hand   (C) the Black Prince goes to
       bleeding.   bed.
   (B) Horatio sees Achilles   (D) Hector appears sad and
       weeping.   ashamed.

6 Lines 15 to 20 portray examples of
   (A) paradox and climax.   (C) climax and irony.
   (B) anticlimax and irony.   (D) none of the above.

7 The title from among these four which would best suit the poem
  is
   (A) Dreaming.   (C) Happy Adventure.
   (B) Feigned Courage.   (D) Brave Achilles.

8 The poet is writing in
   (A) a serious mood.   (C) a persuasive mood.
   (B) a satirical mood.   (D) a nostalgic mood.

9 Which of these statements might best apply to this poem?
   (A) He had the last laugh.   (C) Time marched on.
   (B) Charity began at home.   (D) Fearlessness was only skin
                                       deep.

10 In the last two lines of the poem, the names mentioned really
   refer to
   (A) one person – Horatio.   (C) Edward.
   (B) the three separate heroes. (D) the cowardly French.

11 This poem can be classed as
   (A) sadly reflective.   (C) sweetly lyrical.
   (B) sentimentally descriptive. (D) humorously narrative.

12 Explain the relationships betweeen the earlier and later parts of
   the poem.

13 Is the tone of the poem aptly suited to the subject matter or not?
   Explain why or why not.

14 What particular emotion was aroused in you from reading this
   poem? Do you think it was what the poet intended you to feel?

And there is an anger
In that bronze patience
Tied to the murmur of his fingers.
Those speaking eyes,
5   Squatting on me,
Take up my helplessness
Against his communal gestures.
An apologetic fidget in the chair
Adjusts his harshness.

10   He is a son of the soil who roves
The outskirts of our jungle;
He is our brother who moves
With the sun so easily.
Still,

15   His eyes have strange fires.
Will there be time,
For us, for me
Groping for a neutral gentleness
To reach him without burning,
To lift into laughter?

EDWIN THUMBOO

---

1 'Speaking eyes' (line 4) tells us that
  (A) the poet can tell that the man is intelligent.
  (B) the two people are conversing face to face.
  (C) the man is communicating with the poet in sign language.
  (D) the poet feels the man is thoughtful as he looks at him.

2 Which of the following reveals the poet's mood in the first stanza?
   (A) confidence   (C) disinterest
   (B) diffidence   (D) distrust

3 The phrase 'a son of the soil' means
   (A) a farmer.   (C) a forester.
   (B) a native.   (D) a farmer's son.

4 In this poem, the situation is as follows:
   (A) One person is studying a   (C) Two people are talking
       bronze statue.   and laughing together.
   (B) The poet regards a man   (D) The poet regards another
       angrily.   longingly.

5 Onomatopoeia is used
   (A) in line 10.   (C) in line 3.
   (B) in line 5.   (D) in line 19.

6 The last line of the poem tells us that the poet
   (A) has been laughing at the   (C) wishes to change the mood
       man all along.   of the man through
   (B) intends to lift the man and   contact.
       carry him to safety.   (D) wants to tell the man a
                                         joke.

7 Which two lines tell us that the poet glimpses a momentary
  softening of the man's apparent attitude?
   (A) lines 17 and 18   (C) lines 8 and 9
   (B) lines 6 and 7   (D) lines 4 and 5

8 Which of the following words is NOT used figuratively?
   (A) burning (line 20)   (C) murmur (line 3)
   (B) harshness (line 9)   (D) squatting (line 5)

9 Which phrase best summarises the theme?
   (A) new-found joy   (C) hurt pride
   (B) hoping against hope   (D) undue suffering

10 The poet employs all of the following devices EXCEPT
   (A) rhetorical question.   (C) alliteration.
   (B) simile.   (D) metaphor.

11 Which person in the poem do you empathize with more? Why?

12 Find some other themes besides the dominant one and examine
   how they relate to the latter.

13 Explain why the poet has placed the word 'Still' in the second
   stanza when it could, more naturally, have been put in stanza
   three.

By sundown we came to a hidden village
Where all the air was still
And no sound met our tired ears, save
For the sorry drip of rain from blackened trees
5 And the melancholy song of swinging gates.
Then through a broken pane some of us saw
A dead bird in a rusting cage, still
Pressing his thin tattered breast against the bars,
His beak wide open. And
10 As we hurried through the weed-grown street,
A gaunt dog started up from some dark place
And shambled off on legs as thin as sticks
Into the wood, to die at least in peace.
No-one had told us victory was like this;
15 Not one amongst us would have eaten bread
Before he'd filled the mouth of the grey child
That sprawled, stiff as a stone, before the shattered door.
There was not one who did not think of home.

HENRY TREECE

---

1 The 'we' of the poem are
 (A) soldiers.   (C) criminals.
 (B) health officials.   (D) tourists.

2 The word 'save' (line 3) can be replaced by
 (A) and.   (C) except.
 (B) here.   (D) not.

3 Lines 15 and 16 reveal an attitude of
  (A) callousness.   (C) indifference.
  (B) compassion.   (D) childishness.

4 The 'we' of the poem
  (A) have been defeated in   (C) are the conquerors of
      battle.   battle.
  (B) have returned to their   (D) had no connection
      home in the village.   whatsoever with what had
                                    taken place in the village.

5 In line 14 the speaker
  (A) is filled with the thrill of (C) regrets that he has lost the
      victory.   war.
  (B) is prepared for what he   (D) questions victory's darker
      encounters.   side.

6 Which words suggest that the village had not just (timewise) been
  destroyed?
  (A) 'tattered' and 'broken'   (C) 'rusting' and 'weed-grown'
      (lines 8 and 6)   (lines 7 and 10)
  (B) 'dead' and 'peace' (lines 7 (D) 'blackened' and 'sprawled'
      and 13)   (lines 4 and 17)

7 A simile is used in
  (A) line 5.   (C) line 10.
  (B) line 13.   (D) line 17.

8 Which of the following words is used figuratively?
  (A) 'song' (line 5)   (C) 'shambled' (line 12)
  (B) 'shattered' (line 17)   (D) 'hidden' (line 1)

9 Onomatopoeia is used in
  (A) line 3.   (C) line 4.
  (B) line 6.   (D) line 8.

10 The tone of the poem as a whole is one of
  (A) pity.   (C) aggression.
  (B) elation.   (D) unforgiveness.

11 Give reasons why what is stated in the last line was so.

12 Why were the trees 'blackened'?

13 Comment on the effectiveness of the sentence construction of the
final line of the poem.

14 State the ideas which you think the poet is trying to communicate
by means of the scene which he presents in the poem.

15 Show how the mood of the poem is manifested through the many
images employed.

Earth has not anything to show more fair:
Dull would he be of soul who could pass by
A sight so touching in its majesty:
This City now doth, like a garment, wear
5 The beauty of the morning; silent, bare,
Ships, towers, domes, theatres, and temples lie
Open unto the fields, and to the sky;
All bright and glittering in the smokeless air.
Never did sun more beautifully steep
10 In his first splendour, valley, rock, or hill;
Ne'er saw I, never felt, a calm so deep!
The river glideth at his own sweet will:
Dear God! the very houses seem asleep;
And all that mighty heart is lying still!

WILLIAM WORDSWORTH

1 The scene in the poem is
   (A) a busy one.   (C) a moonlit one.
   (B) a silent one.   (D) a noisy one.

2 The poet is greatly
   (A) saddened by what he sees.   (C) dulled by the scene.
   (B) confused by the sight.   (D) moved by the scene.

3 What time of day is it?
   (A) twilight   (C) sunrise
   (B) noontide   (D) midnight

4 According to the poet
   (A) there are many lovelier   (C) this sight is hardly
       sights on earth.   impressive.
   (B) this is the most beautiful   (D) this is a dull and soulless
       sight on earth.   picture.

5 The poet appeals most strongly to our sense of
   (A) sight.   (C) hearing.
   (B) smell.   (D) touch.

6 The word 'steep' (line 9) means
   (A) shine.   (C) bathe.
   (B) destroy.   (D) climb.

7 The pervading atmosphere of the poem is one of
   (A) immense gaiety.   (C) total alarm.
   (B) absolute boredom.   (D) profound calm.

8 The poet employs all of the following EXCEPT
   (A) personification.   (C) simile.
   (B) onomatopoeia.   (D) hyperbole.

9 Which line best suggests the other face of the city?
   (A) line 3.   (C) line 10.
   (B) line 12.   (D) line 14.

10 The poet describes as 'dull of soul' the man who
   (A) would be unimpressed by   (C) cannot ignore this
       the scene.   touching scene.
   (B) has never come across   (D) would be moved by the
       such a sight before.   scene.

11 What is the poet's intention in this poem?

12 Have you experienced such a setting as is described in the poem? What effect did it have on you?

13 Identify two devices and say how they help to create the prevailing mood of the poem.

14 Try and phrase as best as you can the central theme of the poem.

Turn sideways now and let them see
What loveliness escapes the schools,
Then turn again, and smile, and be
The perfect answer to those fools
5   Who always prate of Greece and Rome,
'The face that launched a thousand ships,'
And such like things, but keep tight lips
For burnished beauty nearer home.
Turn in the sun, my love, my love!
10   What palm-like grace! What poise! I swear
I prize these dusky limbs above my life.
What laughing eyes! What gleaming hair!

H. A. VAUGHAN

1 In the poem the poet
  (A) criticises a student.   (C) admires a young woman.
  (B) talks to a young boy.   (D) talks about a palm tree.

2 He wishes the one addressed in the poem
  (A) would remain silent.   (C) were from Greece or
  (B) were lovelier and wiser.   Rome.
                           (D) to be seen in profile.

3 'Those fools' (line 4) refers to persons
  (A) who are unschooled.   (C) who belong to the poet's
  (B) who come from Greece   region.
      and Rome.   (D) who deny the beauty of
                             the person being
                             addressed.

4 Lines 5 to 8 contain an example of
   (A) simile.   (C) personification.
   (B) onomatopoeia.   (D) antithesis.

5 Line 6 is a reference to
   (A) the person addressed.   (C) those who prate of Rome.
   (B) Helen of Troy.   (D) the poet.

6 'But keep tight lips. . .home' means
   (A) but ignore the kind of   (C) but save their praise for
       beauty around them.   the beauty around them.
   (B) but do not smile when at   (D) but talk of faraway places.
       home.

7 In this poem, the poet
   (A) only praises.   (C) both praises and criticizes.
   (B) only criticises.   (D) does none of the above.

8 'Dusky' (line 11) means
   (A) healthy.   (C) young and tender.
   (B) dark in colour.   (D) white.

9 The poet tends towards exaggeration in
   (A) line 1.   (C) line 11.
   (B) line 7.   (D) line 8.

10 Why might the title 'Revelation' be appropriate to this poem?
   Because
   (A) it has Biblical overtones.   (C) the poet's viewpoint is
   (B) the poet informs on a little   widely held and
       appreciated fact.   appreciated.
                                        (D) the poet has little to say
                                            to us.

11 The dominant theme of the poem is
   (A) happiness in Nature.   (C) never give up.
   (B) a home away from home.   (D) unsung beauty.

12 Can you identify personally with the sentiments expressed by the
   poet? Why, and in what way?

13 What specific point is the poet making?

14 From your own experience of people's attitudes to beauty,
   give some examples of 'and such like things' (line 7).

15 Is the poet concerned only with the beauty of the person
   addressed in the poem? Explain.

Long had I thought
  Of death
And then they told me
You were dead.
I had seen him
Sitting in the ante-room
Eager to be summoned,
So when I heard
You had received him
I was silent.

I went to see you
Lying in death's embrace.
I was afraid —
I thought the sight
Would tear my heart
To pieces,
And my anger would rise
Against death the intruder.

But when I looked
Into your lovely face
And saw the sweet peace
That his kiss
Had implanted,
I could not weep,
And I could not be angry.

Ah, sweet is death,
And kindly,
To those who suffer
Unbearable agony:
Sweet was death's kiss
Upon your lips —
Beloved one
To whom
He gave His Peace.

UNA MARSON

1 To whom does 'him' (line 5) refer?
 (A) a lover   (C) God
 (B) an enemy   (D) death

2 The poet suggests that the 'you' of the poem had a hand in the
 timing of his or her death, in
 (A) stanza 2.   (C) stanza 1.
 (B) stanza 3.   (D) stanza. 4.

3 The figure of speech employed to describe death is
 (A) a simile.   (C) personification.
 (B) a metaphor.   (D) onomatopoeia.

4 In the poem, the poet experiences
 (A) one emotion throughout.   (C) changing emotions.
 (B) only negative emotions.   (D) only positive emotions.

5 The idea of death as a release from pain is expressed in
 (A) stanza 4.   (C) stanza 1.
 (B) stanza 2.   (D) line 6.

6 In the poem, the poet
 (A) is surprised to learn of the   (C) has been expecting the
     death.   death to take place.
 (B) is expecting to be pleased   (D) never expresses fear.
     by what he sees of death.

7 The turning point comes in
 (A) line 10.   (C) line 26.
 (B) line 14.   (D) line 19.

8 The word 'implanted' means
 (A) decorated.   (C) released slowly.
 (B) fixed deeply.   (D) brought about.

9 The overriding mood of the poem is one of
 (A) gross disappointment.   (C) surprised relief.
 (B) deep hurt.   (D) expected sadness.

10 In the last line of the poem, 'He' is used in reference to
 (A) God.   (C) a loved one.
 (B) death.   (D) the poet.

11 How would you express the theme of this poem?

12 If the poet had encountered an opposite picture of the dead
 person, which lines in the poem would have been fulfilled?

13 Compare and contrast some of the thoughts on death in Walcott's
 poem with those in this one.

14 How did you respond to this poem as it developed? Give reasons
 for your answer.

37

PART TWO

Remember to ask yourself questions as you read the poems, following the guidelines given on p.ix — the *who*, *what*, *where*, *when*, *why* and *how*. Think about who is speaking and to whom, and the type of people they are. Look at the setting (time, place and occasion) and the use of language. Consider the main purpose behind the poem, the poet's intention in writing it, and the main idea conveyed. A good way of doing this is to write a short but full restatement of the poem in ordinary prose.

Jamaican Fisherman

Across the sand I saw a black man stride
    To fetch his fishing gear and broken things,
And silently that splendid body cried
    Its proud descent from ancient chiefs and kings.
Across the sand I saw him naked stride;
    Sang his black body in the sun's white light
The velvet coolness of dark forests wide,
    The blackness of the jungle's starless night.
He stood beside the old canoe which lay
Upon the beach; swept up within his arms
The broken nets and careless lounged away
Towards his wretched hut beneath the palms,
Nor knew how fiercely spoke his body then
Of ancient wealth and freeborn regal men.

SIR PHILIP SHERLOCK

1 With what kind of eyes does the poet regard the fisherman?

2 Point out as many uses of contrast in the poem as you can.

3 Does the fisherman express any particular emotion in the poem?

4 Pick out the lines which tell us that the fisherman is or is not conscious of what the poet sees.

5 Explain what the poet sees in the fisherman.

6 What is the main intention of the poet?

7 Pick out a couple of themes from the poem and discuss them.

8 Comment on the poet's use of 'cried', 'sang', and 'spoke'.

9 Are you able to feel as the poet does about the man? If so, what helps you to do so; and if not, why not?

Academic

How sad, they think, to see him homing nightly
In converse with himself across the quad,
Down by the river and the railway arch
To his gaunt villa and his bickering brood,
5   Their mother anchored by a hill of mending.
Such banal feelings – how they pity him.

By day his food is Plato, Machiavelli.
'Thought is a flower, gentlemen,' he says –
Tracing the thought in air until it grows
10   Like frost-flowers on the windows of the mind –
'Thought is a flower that has its roots in dung.'

What irony, they think, that one so nourished,
Perfect in all the classic commonwealths,
Himself so signally should lack the arts
15   To shine and burgeon in the College councils,
A worn-out battery, a nobody, a windbag.
'And yet,' they sigh, 'what has the old boy got,
That every time he talks he fills the hall?'

JAMES REEVES

1 Who is the 'he' of the poem likely to be? Who might the 'they' of the poem be?

2 What emotion do they feel for him? Find the best word.

3 Does the word 'incongruous' have any meaning for the poem? Explain fully.

4 Discuss the image in line 5. Try to compose one of your own for 'a teacher with lots and lots of exercise books to correct for the next morning'. Don't use the same words as the poet.

5 Discuss the use of the word 'nourished' (line 12). Find other examples of figurative language and comment on their effectiveness.

6 Spell out the various aspects of the irony in stanza 3.

7 In your own words, write in prose a short character sketch of the academic.

A Solution

The world contains so many beautiful things to gaze at
That gazing is an occupation that you could spend days at,
And these beautiful things are of so many different kinds, or
    shall we say heterogeneous,
5 Such as the sun and moon etc. and butterflies and mermaids etc.
    that to list them all you would have to be an etcetera genius
So I shall hasten to a landing
And mention two beautiful things that are to my mind outstanding,
And one of them is to be on a train,
10 And see what we see when we flatten our noses against the pane,
And the other is wistful enough to make anybody feel cosmic and
    pious,
Which is to stand beside the track and wave at the passengers as
    they rocket by us,
15 So that is why rather than be an etcetera or any other kind of genius
I would rather be schizophrenious,
Because I should regard it as the most satisfactory of stunts
To be able to split my personality and be in two places at once,
For who could be so happy as I
20 Sitting with my nose against a train window watching me wave to
    me as I go rocketing by?

OGDEN NASH

1 In what mood is the poet writing?

2 What do you think his purpose is?

3 What does the poet mean by saying 'So I shall hasten to a landing'
   (line 7)?

4 Which word is 'coined' by the poet? For what reasons? What
   should it be? What specifically does it relate to in the poem's
   content?

Flowers

I have never learnt the names of flowers.
From beginning, my world has been a place
Of pot-holed streets where thick, sluggish gutters race
In slow time, away from garbage heaps and sewers,
5   Past blanched old houses around which cowers
Stagnant earth. There, scarce green thing grew to chase
The dull-grey squalor of sick dust; no trace
Of plant save few sparse weeds; just these, no flowers.

One day they cleared a space and made a park
10 There in the city's slums; and suddenly
Came stark glory like lightning in the dark,
While perfume and bright petals thundered slowly.
I learnt no names, but hue, shape and scent mark
My mind, even now, with symbols holy.

DENNIS CRAIG

---

1 What impression is the author trying to give us of the scene in the first stanza?

2 Where does the change of scene come? What is the poet's attitude to it? Is he describing two different places?

3 Examine the simile '. . . like lightning in the dark'. (line 11) What qualities of lightning are relevant for this particular image?

4 Give the rhyme scheme of the poem.

5 What particular fact about the poet's experience does not change in the poem?

6 What do you think the flowers symbolise in this poem?

7 Where is it suggested that the poet is speaking quite some time after the event?

8 Discuss these pictures: sick dust; gutters race in slow time; blanched old houses. What feelings are they intended to evoke?

9 How would you read the first section of the poem? Happily or sadly? Quickly or slowly? Why? And the second section?

10 Why didn't the poet feel it necessary to learn the names of flowers even after the change?

Sonnet

Shall I compare thee to a summer's day?
Thou art more lovely and more temperate.
Rough winds do shake the darling buds of May,
And summer's lease hath all too short a date.
5 Sometime too hot the eye of heaven shines,
And often is his gold complexion dimmed;
And every fair from fair sometime declines,
By chance, or nature's changing course, untrimmed;
But thy eternal summer shall not fade,
10 Nor lose possession of that fair thou ow'st,
Nor shall Death brag thou wand'rest in his shade,
When in eternal lines to time thou grow'st.
    So long as men can breathe or eyes can see,
    So long lives this, and this gives life to thee.

WILLIAM SHAKESPEARE

1 To whom is the poet speaking?

2 What is Shakespeare's conclusion about this person *vis-à-vis* a summer's day?

3 What negative aspects of summer does the poet mention?

4 Find three examples of personification in the poem.

5 Is 'thy eternal summer' used literally or figuratively? What qualities does the poet conjure up by the use of that phrase?

6 What is meant by line 11?

7 How does the poet explain the statement he has made in line 11?

8 To what does the 'this' in the last line refer? In what way is the poet paying himself a compliment?

9 Try writing a very flattering poem about somebody or something using the kind of denying comparisons that Shakespeare has used. Keep yours simple.

The Lesson

'Your father's gone,' my bald headmaster said.
His shiny dome and brown tobacco jar
Splintered at once in tears. It wasn't grief.
I cried for knowledge which was bitterer
5 Than any grief. For there and then I knew
That grief has uses — that a father dead
Could bind the bully's fist a week or two;
And then I cried for shame, then for relief.

I was a month past ten when I learnt this:
10 I still remember how the noise was stilled
In school-assembly when my grief came in.
Some goldfish in a bowl quietly sculled
Around their shining prison on its shelf.
They were indifferent. All the other eyes
15 Were turned towards me. Somewhere in myself
Pride, like a goldfish, flashed a sudden fin.

EDWARD LUCIE-SMITH

---

1 Where is the poem set?

2 Explain the phrase 'splintered at once in tears'. Who or what does it relate to? Is it literal or figurative?

3 What does the poet mean by 'grief has uses'? What might have led him to that conclusion?

4 Why does the poet cry for shame? What is he relieved about?

5 What contrast is highlighted in stanza 2?

6 Why is the poem called 'The Lesson'?

7 Try to explain the feeling of pride which the poet experiences. Talk about the image used and its effect.

8 Why is the knowledge (stanza 1) 'bitterer than any grief'?

9 Do you think this boy is usually at ease, happy and comfortable in his school? Discuss.

Lunch Hour

Frederick Street
suffocating,
strangled by people.

Stiletto heels
5   stab at the pavement.

In the formica atmosphere
waiters scuttle by
serving diners their noon portion
of air-conditioned aloofness.

10   Waiting
bites hugely
into the time.

At last at the elbow
a waiter
15   with his 'Instant Coffee' smile.

They've tried to make
that awkward dark cell
below the staircase
into a romantic alcove
20   but
eating there alone
as she always does
the young girl barricades
herself behind a stare
25   hard as old toast.

Going back
the balding city square
smells of dust, detachment
and passions discarded
30   like cheap coats.

JUDY MILES

1 What sort of atmosphere is created in the first five lines?

2 What 'waiting' is referred to (line 10)?

3 Do you like the poet's use of images? Why or why not?

4 Make a list of all the non-literal language used between lines 1 and 15. Examine its meanings and effect.

5 Suggest reasons why lines 23 to 25 might be so.

6 Where do you think the poet is? Is it she talking in the poem or is it the young girl?

7 Why 'the balding city square'?

8 Find two examples of the use of similes and say how they relate to the theme and tone of the poem.

9 Talk about some of the lunch-time experiences suggested by the last five lines.

10 'Going back' (line 26) where? In your own words say what the poet is talking about in the poem. Try using only one sentence but giving a full answer.

11 Look at these words which have relevance for the poem: 'makeshift', 'superficial', 'temporary', 'insincere'. Find the respective sections to which they might apply.

12 How does the poet's use of short lines help to support or hinder the effect which is created by the words referred to in question 11?

13 What tone is evident in the poem?

Bird

That day the bird hunted an empty, gleaming sky
and climbed and coiled and spun measures of joy,
half-sleeping in the sly wind way
above my friend and me. Oh,
5 its wings' wind-flick and fleche were free
and easy in the sun, and a whip's tip
tracing of pleasure its mute madrigal,
that I below watched it so tall
it could not fall save slow
10 down the slow day.

'What is it?' said my friend.
'Yonder...'
            hill and home patterned and curved
and frozen in the white round air
15 'Yes, there,' he said, 'I see it —'
                   up
the steep sky till the eye
lidded from weight of sun on earth and wing!

'Watch this,' he said, bending for stones,
20 and my boy's throat grew tight with warning
to the bird that rode the feathered morning.

'Now there's a good shot, boy!' he said.
I was only ten then.
'If you see any more be sure to shout
25 but don't look at the sun too long,' he said,
'makes your eyes run.'

DENNIS SCOTT

1 Lines 1 to 10 describe the flight of the bird in the poem. Try to find some of your own words to suggest the manner in which the bird was flying.

2 Is the bird aware of any danger or sadness?

3 Are both boys looking at the bird in lines 1 to 10? How do you know?

4 Find a strong alliterative line in the poem.

5 Where does the change of language and mood first arise? Account for the change of pattern in the second half of the poem.

6 Where do we get the impression of a camera focusing on one scene and refocusing on another scene to highlight the connection between the two?

7 What sets of emotion are experienced in the poem?

8 The poet was only ten. Do you think the other person was much younger, much older or what? Give evidence for your answer.

9 Does the last line of the poem have any significance beyond just its face value? Were the boy's eyes running at all? from the sun?

Road to Lacovia

This is a long forbidding road, a narrow,
hard aisle of asphalt under
a high gothic arch of bamboos.
Along it a woman drags a makeshift barrow
5   in slanting rain, and thunder:
a thin woman who wears no shoes.

This is St Elizabeth, a hard parish
to work: but when you are born
10   on land, you want to work that land.
Nightfall comes here swift and harsh and deep, but garish
flames of lightning show up torn
cheap clothing barely patched, and

a face patterned by living. Every sharp line
15   of this etching has the mark
of struggle. To the eye, unyielding
bleak earth has brought her close to famine;
yet through this wild descent of dark
this woman dares to walk, and sing.

A. L. HENDRIKS

---

1 Look up the meanings of 'gothic' and 'etching' and then discuss the poet's use of these words.

2 Who is the person in the poem, where is she, and what is she doing?

3 Go through each stanza and list the qualities of hardness shown up everywhere and in everything.

4 How do these bring out the character of the person being described?

5 Examine all the likely reasons for the poet's use of 'aisle' (line 2).

6 Why exactly has this person had to struggle? In which stanza is the reason revealed?

7 How does this woman react to her circumstances? Talk about the use of 'dares'.

8 Where does a change of mood and tone come?

9 Is there, finally, any touch of 'softness' in the manner in which the woman rises above her situation?

10 Did you feel what the poet hoped you would feel about the woman? If so, what helped you to do so?

In the Gentle Afternoon

Such commerce
for a small village without a representative
on Central Government, without a village council,
without a working public toilet, with two
5   stand pipes, three rum shops and a cricket pitch;
such business
as citizens sit on benches and discuss
the latest test scores, last night's trouble
at the dance, Sunday's chance in the rounders match
10 the price of cod fish, the problems of cross week;
such activity
late in the afternoon on Friday as mother
rushes over to seize her child; boys plot;
a girl shouts her directions, a jeep coughs
15 to a standstill by the shop, and erupts an eager crowd;
such peace
in the gentle afternoon, as the sun begins to die
and everybody drifts away to attend their affairs
all part of the village family, all private people
20 with each a share of secrets, known by all.

ROYSTON ELLIS

---

1 Discuss the many features of the village (explicit and implicit)
which the poet presents.

2 Can you identify any turning points in this poem? Of what
significance are they?

3 What literary device is used in the phrase 'secrets, known by all'
(line 20), and how does it effectively emphasise the nature of the
village setting?

4 Note how the poet introduces each section of the poem. Why do
you think he repeats that style? What effect does it produce?

5 What time of the afternoon is described as 'gentle' in the poem?

6 Comment on the effectiveness of the poet's use of 'coughs' (line
14). What figures of speech are employed here? How do they suit
the mood at that point in the poem?

7 Is your neighbourhood or village anything like the one presented
in this poem? In a paragraph, discuss its similarities and/or
differences.

Canes by the Roadside

Time was
you tossed in a delirium
of whispers near the roadside:
now your last whisper
5   is a treasury of lost sound.

Months ago
you were a handful
of green ribbons teasing the wind:
now dead strips tell
10   where the colour and the sparkle go.

In the cycle
of things you will submit
to the tyranny of shining teeth
and the remorseless murmur of the mill
15   and all your once-green pride will not console a bit.

Heaped up
in your pyre ready for
the yearly sacrifices to power
you lie robbed of the majesty
20   of your plotted earth
bared of the eagerness of your dream.

                           A. N. FORDE

1 In one sentence, say what this poem is essentially about. Start off in this way: 'In this poem, the poet. . .'

2 What two senses are appealed to through the description of the canes in stanzas 1 and 2 respectively?

3 Examine the images in terms of mood and meaning of the poem and discuss their effect, e.g. 'tossed in a delirium', 'teasing the wind'.

4 Note the three times mentioned in the poem. Which lines refer to which times?

5 At the start of the poem what mood is given to the canes? And at what time of their being? Where are the mood and time repeated?

6 Discuss some of the themes present in the poem. The central one concerns 'changing fortunes', but there are sub-themes to be found in the various stanzas.

7 Is the poet's attitude towards the fate of the canes evident? Support your answer.

8 Where do we learn what will happen in the future to the canes? What words suggest the inevitability of their fate?

The Muse's Complaint

Albertina say:
I want some other rhythm
dis one cyah make me
break away
5   an' I tired dancing waltz.
Look dey!
You see dem children?
if I only coulda
rock like dey rock
10   (and den)
dip back and jerk
(like dem)
you know I woulda
free up me mind,
15   is such a long time
I want feel like myself
again.

some other rhythm
some other rhythm

20   I doan want to tell lies
just the truth as it is
woulda alright wid me
but i cyah hear it right

(some other rhythm
25   some other rhythm)

Albertina, Albertina say:
I want some other rhythm
because dis one too light
dem make it too tight
30   it noh free
it eh me
it too slow
it cyah show
all the things that I be
35   so
I want some other rhythm
dat will free up me senses
break down de fences
(just take a look at dem
40   children dancing)
some other rhythm
dat goin' rock to de bottom
of me.

                    KENDEL HIPPOLYTE

1 How many kinds of dance or rhythm are talked about in this poem?

2 Match them to the past, present and future of the poem.

3 Discuss how the poet uses these rhythms to progress through the stages of his poem and develop his theme.

4 Think about how the poet uses each of these dances to illustrate and represent something much bigger and more serious than itself. In other words, the symbolism. Explain the symbolism of each rhythm starting with the waltz.

5 The poet uses children's dancing to contrast with his own. What qualities typically present in children are able to put them ahead of him in this context?

6 You may have thought from your first reading that this poem was really about dancing and nothing more – and that's quite acceptable. Now that you have explored it in greater depth, however, make sure you are aware of how much you may have underestimated the poet's intention in this and other poems that you read.

The Fox and the Cat

The fox and the cat, as they travelled one day,
With moral discourses cut shorter the way:
''Tis great,' says the fox, 'to make justice our guide!'
'How god-like is mercy!' Grimalkin replied.
5   Whilst thus they proceeded, a wolf from the wood,
Impatient of hunger, and thirsting for blood,
Rushed forth — as he saw the dull shepherd asleep —
And seized for his supper an innocent sheep.
'In vain, wretched victim, for mercy you bleat.
10 When mutton's at hand,' says the wolf, 'I must eat.'
       Grimalkin's astonished! — the fox stood aghast,
To see the fell beast at his bloody repast.
'What a wretch,' says the cat, ''Tis the vilest of brutes;
Does he feed upon flesh when there's herbage and roots?'
15 Cries the fox, 'While our oaks give us acorns so good,
What a tyrant is this to spill innocent blood!'
       Well, onward they marched, and they moralized still
Till they came where some poultry picked chaff by a mill;
Sly Reynard surveyed them with gluttonous eyes,
20 And made, spite of morals, a pullet his prize.
A mouse, too, that chanced from her covert to stray,
The greedy Grimalkin secured as her prey.
       A spider that sat in her web on the wall,
Perceived the poor victims, and pitied their fall;
25 She cried, 'Of such murders, how guiltless am I!'
So ran to regale on a new-taken fly.

JAMES VINCENT CUNNINGHAM

---

1 Explain what is meant in line 2.

2 What word tells us that the first victim pleaded for his life?

3 What is the meaning of 'repast'?

4 The cat and the fox thought there was ample opportunity for the wolf to be ve – – – – – – n.

5 Restate line 20 in your own words.

6 Does the word 'hypocrisy' have meaning in the context of the poem? Find other words to label the behaviour of the fox, cat and spider.

7 What type of poem is this?

8 What is the poet's intention? Is it merely to amuse, or to tell us something serious about ourselves, or both?

9 Find some proverbs which have application for the poem. There is one about throwing stones. There are others.

The Send-off

Down the close, darkening lanes they sang their way
To the siding-shed,
And lined the train with faces grimly gay.

Their breasts were stuck all white with wreath and spray
5   As men's are, dead.

Dull porters watched them, and a casual tramp
Stood staring hard,
Sorry to miss them from the upland camp.
Then, unmoved, signals nodded, and a lamp
10   Winked to the guard.

So secretly, like wrongs hushed-up, they went.
They were not ours:
We never heard to which front these were sent.

Nor there if they yet mock what women meant
15   Who gave them flowers.

Shall they return to beatings of great bells
In wild train-loads?
A few, a few, too few for drums and yells,
May creep back, silent, to village wells
Up half-known roads.

WILFRED OWEN

---

1   Who do you think the 'they' of the poem are?

2   Explain the antithetical element of 'grimly gay' (line 3).

3   Why does the poet say, 'They were not ours' (line 12)? Were they
not from the same country as the poet?

4   Do you like the simile in line 11? Would it have universal appeal?
Is it effective?

5   Give examples of indifference and caring in the poem.

6   Comment on the use of 'nodded' (line 9) and 'winked' (line 10).

7   Compare the departure with the anticipated return.

8   How would you describe the last stanza of the poem? What sort of
mood is the poet in at the end? Give more than one possible
answer.

9   What are your own feelings on war?

If I have Sinned in Act

If I have sinned in act, I may repent;
If I have erred in thought, I may disclaim
My silent error, and yet feel no shame —
But if my soul, big with an ill intent,
5 Guilty in will, by fate be innocent,
Or being bad, yet murmurs at the curse
And incapacity of being worse
That makes my hungry passion still keep Lent
In keen expectance of a Carnival;
10 Where, in all worlds, that round the sun revolve
And shed their influence on this passive ball,
Abides a power that can my soul absolve?
Could any sin survive, and be forgiven —
One sinful wish would make a hell of heaven.

HARTLEY COLERIDGE

---

1 What, in Coleridge's estimation, is the unpardonable sin?

2 Lines 8 and 9 contain some effective images. What do Lent and Carnival represent? In your own words explain the meaning of these lines.

3 What device is used in lines 10 to 12? What effect does it have?

4 What is the aim of the poet in this poem?

5 In what tone of voice does he write?

6 The poet makes much use of antithesis throughout. Show how this helps to create the overall meaning or mood of the poem.

7 How did you respond to the poet's expression of personal emotion? Explain.

Ancestor on the Auction Block

Ancestor on the auction block
Across the years your eyes seek mine
Compelling me to look.
I see your shackled feet
Your primitive black face
I see your humiliation
And turn away
Ashamed.

Across the years your eyes seek mine
Compelling me to look
Is this mean creature that I see
Myself?
Ashamed to look
Because of myself ashamed
Shackled by my own ignorance
I stand
A slave.

Humiliated
I cry to the eternal abyss
For understanding
Ancestor on the auction block
Across the years your eyes meet mine
Electric
I am transformed
My freedom is within myself.

I look you in the eyes and see
The spirit of God eternal
Of this only need I be ashamed
Of blindness to the God within me
The same God who dwelt within you
The same eternal God
Who shall dwell
In generations yet unborn.

Ancestor on the auction block
Across the years
I look
I see your sweating, toiling, suffering
Within your loins I see the seed
Of multitudes
From your labour
Grow roads, aqueducts, cultivation
A new country is born
Yours was the task to clear the ground
Mine be the task to build.

VERA BELL

1 Why are the feet of the poet's ancestor shackled?

2 Where is the turning point in the poem and what specifically does it represent for the poet?

3 Find the words which the poet repeats to describe both herself and her ancestor. To what effect?

4 Of what only need the poet feel ashamed?

5 What does she consider was the contribution made by her ancestor? How does she establish a logical link between the two of them?

6 Read the poem aloud, giving emphasis to the one-word lines, pausing before them, using various readers and voices.

7 In which stanza is irony given full sway? Discuss.

8 Make a summary of the ideas in the poem. Begin something like this: 'At the start of the poem we see the poet very uncomfortable with her ancestral past.' Now continue, ending with the resolution of the crisis.

9 Into what category would you place this kind of poem, e.g. descriptive, reflective, narrative?

A Wheel Called Progress

When I was sent to school
it was not gadgetry and gimmicks
we were given.
The teacher told you clearly
5   what you had to know
and so you learnt it even though
it had no piston-rod attached to living.
A strait-jacket was all
our flailing minds were held to grow in.

10   For English Language it was verbs and nouns
and for Geography promontories
and names of towns.
None of my teachers was at liberty
to help me use the bricks of words
15   to build a dome to house experience.
None thought the axis of Geography
was Man.

Then some acknowledged Dewey
had just uncovered a
20   long-buried key
that turned the door to
better learning through
discovery.
And for a time
25   the minds of lucky children
were set free.

But soon the adoration
of machinery
made quick abortion
30   of that prophet's theory
about the road we tread
to human dignity,
so cranks installed instead
gleaming technology
35   and now we dance among
shining gadgetry
disguised gimmickry
programmed learning and
objective battery;
40   those modern instruments to put
the minds of children back
into strait-jackets
where they belong.

CECIL GRAY

1 How does the poet feel about what was taught and how it was taught in his schooldays?

2 What is the poet's attitude to what is expressed in lines 13 to 17? How does he feel about Man and Experience?

3 Who do you think Dewey (line 18) must be? What exactly was his contribution? How does the poet regard it?

4 Explain the phrases 'made quick abortion' (line 29) and 'had no piston-rod attached to living' (line 7).

5 What came after Dewey? How does the poet feel about this stage?

6 There are two turning points in the poem. Where do they occur? Which two stages in the development of the idea of the poem do they represent?

7 Is the word 'wheel' in the title appropriate for the poem? Say what qualities of a wheel apply.

8 What is the meaning of 'cranks' (line 33)?

9 Is the last line of the poem said sincerely? If yes, justify. If no, what tone is used to end on and why?

Hawk Roosting

I sit in the top of the wood, my eyes closed.
Inaction, no falsifying dream
Between my hooked head and hooked feet:
Or in a sleep rehearse perfect kills and eat.

5   The convenience of the high trees!
The air's buoyancy and the sun's ray
Are of advantage to me;
And the earth's face upward for my inspection.

My feet are locked upon the rough bark.
10   It took the whole of Creation
To produce my foot, my each feather:
Now I hold Creation in my foot

Or fly up, and revolve it all slowly —
I kill where I please because it is all mine.
15   There is no sophistry in my body:
My manners are tearing off heads —

The allotment of death.
For the one path of my flight is direct
Through the bones of the living.
20   No arguments assert my right:

The sun is behind me.
Nothing has changed since I began.
My eye has permitted no change.
I am going to keep things like this.

TED HUGHES

---

1 Say how the words 'violent', 'conceited', 'permanent',
'omnipotent', 'opportunistic' and 'unyielding', apply to the poem.
Identify a passage in the poem for each.

2 Much of the language used in the poem is straightforward and
direct. Why? How does this add to what the poet wishes to
convey?

3 The poet makes the hawk himself speak, and tell us about his
characteristics. What effect does this have?

4 Knowing the nature of the hawk, and thinking of it as
representing something beyond itself, what real-life situations can
you think of for which this poem might be symbolic?

Before the Scales, Tomorrow

And when the enthusiastic
story of our time
is told,
for those
5   who are yet to be born
but announce themselves
with more generous face,
we will come out ahead
  – those who have suffered most from it.

10   And that
being ahead of your time
means suffering much from it.

But it's beautiful to love the world
with eyes
15   that have not yet
been born.

And splendid
to know yourself victorious
when all around you
20   it's all still so cold,
                so dark.

OTTO RENE CASTILLO

1 On whose behalf is the poet talking when he uses 'we' and 'our'?

2 The poem contains a blend of times – present and future. Which lines relate to which times?

3 What is the relationship between the 'we' of the poem and 'those who are yet to be born' (lines 4 to 5)? Show how it is linked to the two times represented in the poem.

4 How would you describe the self-image of the poet? How does he justify it?

5 Look at the use of images, repetition and rhythm. See how it relates to mood and meaning.

6 What does the word 'scales' symbolise in the title and to which of the two times (in the poem) does it belong?

Light Love

I, remembering how light love
hath a soft footfall, and fleet
that goes clicking down
the heart's lone
5   and empty street
in a kind
of spread twilight-nimbus of the mind,
and a soft voice of shaken laughter
like the wind...

10   I, remembering this,
And remembering that light love is
As fragile as a kiss
Lightly given,
And passes like the little rain
15   softly down-driven...

Bade love come to you
with rough male footsteps –
Deliberate –
That hurt to come,
20   And hurt to go...

And bade love speak to you
With accents terrible, and slow.

ROGER MAIS

_____

66

1 What do you understand by 'light love' in the poem?

2 In your own words and in literal language, describe some of the characteristics of this kind of love according to the poet.

3 Does the poet describe another kind of love in the poem? Where does he introduce this new picture of love?

4 What did the poet expect to achieve with this kind of love?

5 Compare the rhythm in the earlier section of the poem with that of the last seven lines. Say how each relates to the poet's views of love.

6 Complete this statement: 'In this poem, the poet says that in order for...'

7 Do you agree with the point that the poet makes about love? Why or why not?

Flame-heart

So much have I forgotten in ten years,
So much in ten brief years! I have forgot
What time the purple apples come to juice,
And what month brings the shy forget-me-not.
5   I have forgot the special, startling season
Of the pimento's flowering and fruiting;
What time of year the ground doves brown the fields
And fill the noonday with their curious fluting.
I have forgotten much, but still remember
10   The poinsettia's red, blood-red in warm December.

I still recall the honey-fever grass,
But cannot recollect the high days when
We rooted them out of the pingwing path
To stop the mad bees in the rabbit pen.
15   I often try to think in what sweet month
The languid painted ladies used to dapple
The yellow by-road mazing from the main,
Sweet with the golden threads of the rose-apple.
I have forgotten — strange — but quite remember
20   The poinsettia's red, blood-red in warm December.

What weeks, what months, what time of the mild year
We cheated school to have our fling at tops?
What days our wine-thrilled bodies pulsed with joy
Feasting upon blackberries in the copse?
25   Oh some I know! I have embalmed the days,
Even the sacred moments when we played,
All innocent of passion, uncorrupt,
At noon and evening in the flame-heart's shade.
We were so happy, happy, I remember,
30   Beneath the poinsettia's red in warm December.

CLAUDE McKAY

1 What mood is evident in the poem? How do you think this mood is sharpened by the way in which the poet contrasts his memories?

2 What time of his life is being recalled? How do you know?

3 List some of the memories of the poet — things seen, heard and done.

4 What particular fact about each memory (but one) does he not recall?

5 Look at some of the images, e.g. 'brown the fields' (line 7). What does the poet mean? What does he wish us to see? Now discuss other images and their effectiveness. There are several throughout the poem.

6 What is the flame-heart?

7 Why do you think the poet's memory of the experience is so total?

8 Find instances in the poem where he does recall time (of any kind) clearly.

9 Are all the lines said in the same pace and tone? Read the lines which call for a slower, more reflective tone, and account for the difference.

10 Do you like this poem? Say why, or why not.

'Twas Ever Thus

I never rear'd a young gazelle,
    (Because, you see, I never tried);
But had it known and loved me well,
    No doubt the creature would have died.
5 My rich and aged Uncle John
    Has known me long and loves me well,
But still persists in living on —
    I would he were a young gazelle.

I never loved a tree or flower;
10   But, if I had, I beg to say
The blight, the wind, the sun, or shower
    Would soon have withered it away.
I've dearly loved my Uncle John,
    From childhood to the present hour,
15 And yet he will go living on —
    I would he were a tree or flower!

H. S. LEIGH

1 What do you take to be the poet's feelings for his Uncle John?

2 How has he chosen to convey these feelings to us? What tone does he use?

3 Are we to take him absolutely seriously, or not?

4 What type of poem would you say this is? For example, is it reflective, descriptive, humorous, a love poem, or a narrative?

5 What method has the poet employed in the structuring of his content to make his point clear? Does it work well that way? Discuss.

The Riders

Over the hill in the mist of the morning,
I see them a-coming, an army a-wheel;
Four abreast, six abreast, the road keeps on spawning
Them, hard-riding men with faces of steel.

5 Young men and old men, they ride on together,
None paying heed to the one at his side;
Toe to toe; wheel to wheel. Crouched on the leather
Seats, over their handle-bars, onward they ride.

Grim must their faces be; theirs is the ride of life;
10 Bread's at the end of it, and leisure to follow;
Bread for a mother or sister or wife,
A toy for the kid, or a kiss in the Hollow.

Out of the distance and into the view they come,
Hundreds of men with their feet on the pedals;
15 The sweat on their faces; hear how their cycles hum,
Riding for bread, not for glory or medals.

BARNABAS J. RAMON-FORTUNÉ

---

1 Comment on the poet's use of 'spawning' (line 3). What qualities
  are suggested by 'faces of steel' (line 4)?

2 'Toe to toe; wheel to wheel' (line 7): where is the same sort of
  picture suggested earlier?

3 Find as many adjectives (of your own) as you can to describe the
  men through each stanza.

4 Where are the men going? Is this a usual occurrence or not?

5 Explain what the poet means by 'bread's at the end of it' (line 10).

6 Do you agree with the poet that the men's faces must be grim?

7 Do the men make their journey with anyone in mind?

8 Find examples of metaphor, alliteration, antithesis and
  onomatopoeia.

9 Is the poet sympathetic towards the riders or not? Support your
  answer.

10 What kind of rhythm is evident in the poem and how does it
   relate (a) to the mood of the men, and (b) to the theme of the
   poem?

from Ulysses

There lies the port: the vessel puffs her sail:
There gloom the dark broad seas. My mariners,
Souls that have toil'd, and wrought, and thought with me —
That ever with a frolic welcome took
5   The thunder and the sunshine, and opposed
Free hearts, free foreheads — you and I are old;
Old age hath yet his honour and his toil;
Death closes all; but something ere the end,
Some work of noble note, may yet be done,
10 Not unbecoming men that strove with Gods.
The lights begin to twinkle from the rocks:
The long day wanes: the slow moon climbs: the deep
Moans round with many voices. Come, my friends,
'Tis not too late to seek a newer world.
15 Push off, and sitting well in order smite
The sounding furrows; for my purpose holds
To sail beyond the sunset, and the baths
Of all the western stars, until I die.
It may be that the gulfs will wash us down:
20 It may be we shall touch the Happy Isles,
And see the great Achilles, whom we knew.
Tho' much is taken, much abides; and tho'
We are not now that strength which in old days
Moved earth and heaven; that which we are, we are;
25 One equal temper of heroic hearts,
Made weak by time and fate, but strong in will
To strive, to seek, to find, and not to yield.

ALFRED, LORD TENNYSON

The above is an extract from Tennyson's famous poem 'Ulysses', written in blank verse. In it Ulysses is speaking to his men and showing his determination to take to the seas again before he dies. He tries to sell his idea and enthusiasm to his listeners. Note how much antithesis (balancing of contrasting ideas) is made use of. This helps to highlight and underline the point the poet makes in the second half of each antithetical statement, and so to reinforce the overall theme or idea of the poem and its tone.

Read the poem intelligently, more than once, and then examine it further by means of the hints below.

1 Look for lines conveying slow speed, greater speed, great determination, great power.

2 Examine lines of contrasting ideas and see how they work towards Ulysses' goal.

3 Discuss appeals made to persuade, and their effectiveness.

4 Note examples of metaphor, climax, hyperbole, personification and their specific function in the poem.

The above is an extract from Tennyson's famous poem Ulysses, in much blank verse. If it tries is seeking to be trained, showing his determination to take to the sea, read below. He could tell his tale and end phases of his tale over. And how much numbers-followers of overcoming delay is much more . . . this helps to display and here the amount the poet makes in the second half of . . . appropriately arranged, and to together . . . . The overwhelming, one idea of the poem and its tone.

Read the poem carefully, more than once, and understanding it further by means of the hints below.

1 Look for lines conveying slow speed, quiet speed, great / determination, great power.

2 By using lots of commas, the . . . can we how they are trying to Ulysses god?

3 Poems speak itself to persuade, and the effect comes.

4 Note examples of metaphor, simile, hyperbole, personification and their specific use in the poem.

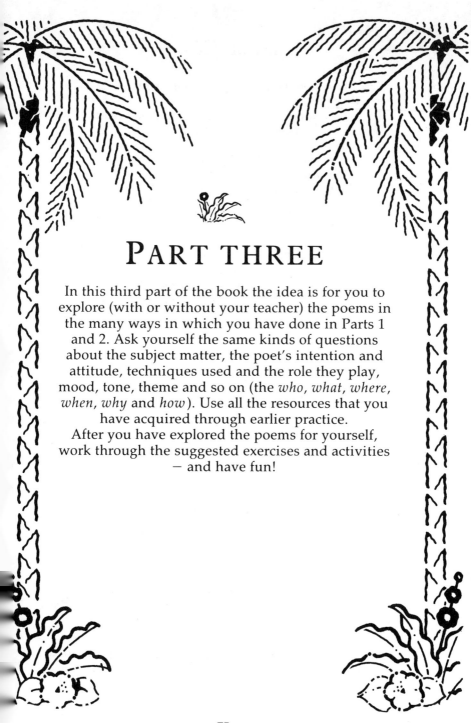

PART THREE

In this third part of the book the idea is for you to
explore (with or without your teacher) the poems in
the many ways in which you have done in Parts 1
and 2. Ask yourself the same kinds of questions
about the subject matter, the poet's intention and
attitude, techniques used and the role they play,
mood, tone, theme and so on (the *who*, *what*, *where*,
when, *why* and *how*). Use all the resources that you
have acquired through earlier practice.
After you have explored the poems for yourself,
work through the suggested exercises and activities
— and have fun!

Carrion Crows

Yes, I have seen them perched on paling posts —
Brooding with evil eyes upon the road,
Their black wings hooded — and they left these roosts
When I have hissed at them. Away they strode
5   Clapping their wings in a man's stride, away
Over the fields. And I have seen them feast
On swollen carrion in the broad eye of day,
Pestered by flies, and yet they never ceased.

But I have seen them emperors of the sky,
10   Balancing gracefully in the wind's drive
With their broad sails just shifting, or again
Throwing huge shadows from the sun's eye
To brush so swiftly over the field's plain,
And winnowing the air like beauty come alive.

A. J. SEYMOUR

1 Compose three short-answer questions on this poem — one to do
with the poet's feelings, another with a selected image of your
choice, and yet another on two different kinds of rhythm used in
the poem and their relationship to what is being talked about in
each case.

2 Rewrite the poem either in the first person singular or first person
plural from the bird's/birds' perspective. Compare and contrast
what you do, from the point of view of tone, mood and intention,
with the poem as written by the poet. Start 'Yes, I have perched
on paling posts...'.

A Small Tragedy

They came up in the evening
And said to him, 'Fly!
All is discovered!'
And he fled.

5   A quiet little man,
Of no importance.
In fifty years he had acquired
Only flat feet and spectacles
And a distressing cough.

10   After a month or more,
(He having gone so quickly)
An inspector called
And they began to find the bodies.

A large number of them,
15   Stuffed into cupboards and corners.
(At work he was tidy
But files and paper-clips
Are matters of some importance.)

In the end, of course,
20   He was hanged,
Very neatly,
Though pleading insanity.

A quiet little man,
Who knew what to do with files and paper-clips,
25   But had no ideas about people
Except to destroy them.

SALLY ROBERTS

---

1 In small groups discuss the poet's tone and her attitude to the man. Use evidence from the poet to support your answers. What do you conclude about the man in the poem? What is the main stylistic feature of the poet's language? Why is the poem called 'A Small Tragedy'?

2 Make up two multiple-choice questions (of four options each) on this poem.

3 If you were the prosecution attorney in the supposed trial of this quiet little man, write your final summation address to the jury in which you hope to convince them that he must hang.

History Makers

I
Women stone breakers
Hammers and rocks
Tired child makers
Haphazard frocks.
5 Strong thigh
Rigid head
Bent nigh
Hard white piles
Of stone
10 Under hot sky
In the gully bed.

II
No smiles
No sigh
No moan.

III
15 Women child bearers
Pregnant frocks
Wilful toil sharers
Destiny shapers
History makers
20 Hammers and rocks.

GEORGE CAMPBELL

1 Think of a group of workers who have a tough job but are not as
appreciated as you think they should be. Write a few lines on a)
them and their surroundings, b) their reaction to their work and
c) how you regard them.

2 Write a paragraph in prose showing how the women might react
to the poet's descriptions of them in the poem as a whole.

Music a Kind of Sleep

Music a kind of sleep
imposes on this weary flesh
wind beyond silence
speech of the God who ordered
5   trees flowering of dark earth
light, essence of darkness
birth.

Lucifer massed
in arrogant disorder all about
10   pale quiet strength of stellar presences
hears in a wonderful dread
music a calm
persistent tread
above the wild torment of nameless waters.

BASIL MCFARLANE

1 Think about another suitable title for the poem. What did you
come up with?

2 Compose three short-answer questions on this poem. Vary the
types of question.

3 Do you share the poet's feelings about music? Illustrate your ideas
in support or rejection of the poet's view.

from Song of Myself

(sections 1 and 2)

1

I celebrate myself,
And what I assume you shall assume,
For every atom belonging to me as good belongs to
    you.

5   I loafe and invite my soul,
I lean and loafe at my ease.... observing a spear of
    summer grass.

2

Houses and rooms are full of perfumes.... the
    shelves are crowded with perfumes,
10   I breathe the fragrance myself, and know it and like
    it,
The distillation would intoxicate me also, but I shall
    not let it.

The atmosphere is not a perfume.... it has no taste
15   of the distillation.... it is odorless,
It is for my mouth forever.... I am in love with it,
I will go to the bank by the wood and become
    undisguised and naked,
I am mad for it to be in contact with me.

20   The smoke of my own breath,
Echoes, ripples, and buzzed whispers.... loveroot,
    silkthread, crotch and vine,

My respiration and inspiration.... the beating of my
    heart.... the passing of blood and air through
    my lungs,
The sniff of green leaves and dry leaves, and of the
    shore and darkcolored sea-rocks, and of hay in
    the barn,
The sound of the belched words of my voice....
30   words loosed to the eddies of the wind,

A few light kisses.... a few embraces.... reaching
    around of arms,
The play of shine and shade on the trees as the
    supple boughs wag,
35   The delight alone or in the rush of the streets, or
    along the fields and hill-sides,
The feeling of health.... the full-noon trill.... the
    song of me rising from bed and meeting the sun.

Have you reckoned a thousand acres much? Have you
40   reckoned the earth much?
Have you practised so long to learn to read?
Have you felt so proud to get at the meaning of
        poems?

Stop this day and night with me and you shall
45   possess the origin of all poems,
You shall possess the good of the earth and sun....
        there are millions of suns left,
You shall no longer take things at second or third
        hand....nor look through the eyes of the dead.
50   ....nor feed on the spectres in books,
You shall not look through my eyes either, nor take
        things from me,
You shall listen to all sides and filter them from
        yourself.

                            WALT WHITMAN

One of America's most famous poets, Walt Whitman writes in free
verse. He often writes about subjects that earlier poets thought were
unsuitable for poetry.

1 What does the poet tell us about himself? How does he make the
   link with us, his readers?

2 In what way is this poem an invitation?

3 Consider what purposes repetition serves, especially in this
   unrhymed poem.

4 Write a letter to the poet telling him how you have responded to
   his invitation and why and how, specifically, you think it will
   benefit you.

Looking at your Hands

No!
I will not still my voice!
I have
too much to claim —
5 if you see me
looking at books
or coming to your house
or walking in the sun
know that I look for fire!

10 I have learnt
from books dear friend
of men dreaming and living
and hungering in a room without a light
who could not die since death was far too poor
15 who did not sleep to dream, but dreamed to change the world

and so
if you see me
looking at your hands
listening when you speak
20 marching in your ranks
you must know
I do not sleep to dream, but dream to change the world.

MARTIN CARTER

1 Study the poem and make notes on how you would arrange it for
   choral speaking with your class. Pay attention to pace, tone,
   volume, solo or group voices. Try out your ideas with your class
   group.

2 Write a conversation between the poet and another person, in
   which the latter disagrees with the poet and protests against much
   of what he is saying. Begin the dialogue with the other person.

Character of a Happy Life

How happy is he born and taught
That serveth not another's will;
Whose armour is his honest thought
And simple truth his utmost skill!

5   Whose passions not his masters are,
Whose soul is still prepared for death,
Not tied unto the world with care
Of public fame, or private breath;

Who envies none that chance doth raise
10   O'r vice; who never understood
How deepest wounds are given by praise;
Nor rules of state, but rules of good:

Who hath his life from rumours freed,
Whose conscience is his strong retreat;
15   Whose state can neither flatterers feed,
Nor ruin make accusers great;

Who God doth late and early pray
More of his grace than gifts to lend;
And entertains the harmless day
20   With a well-chosen book or friend;

– This man is freed from servile bands
Of hope to rise, or fear to fall;
Lord of himself, though not of lands;
And having nothing, yet hath all.

SIR HENRY WOTTON

---

1 Write a paragraph outlining the qualities the poet thinks are sure
to make a man happy and free.

2 Think of some qualities and kinds of behaviour which you feel are
admirable in life and which make a person master of himself.
Write a stanza of poetry about them.

The Best of School

The blinds are drawn because of the sun,
And the boys and the room in a colourless gloom
Of underwater float: bright ripples run
Across the walls as the blinds are blown
5 To let the sunlight in; and I,
As I sit on the shores of the class, alone,
Watch the boys in their summer blouses
As they write, their round heads busily bowed:

And one after another rouses
10 His face to look at me,
To ponder very quickly,
As seeing he does not see.

And then he turns again, with a little glad
Thrill of his work he turns again from me,
15 Having found what he wanted, having got what was to be
    had.

And very sweet it is, while the sunlight waves
In the ripening morning, to sit alone with the class
And feel the stream of awakening ripple and pass
20 From me to the boys, whose brightening souls it laves
For this little hour.

               This morning, sweet it is
To feel the lads' looks light on me,
Then back in a swift, bright flutter to work;
25 Each one darting away with his
Discovery, like birds that steal and flee.

Touch after touch I feel on me
As their eyes glance at me for the grain
Of rigour they taste delightedly.
30 As tendrils reach out yearningly,
Slowly rotate till they touch the tree
That they cleave unto, and up which they climb
Up to their lives — so they to me.

I feel them cling and cleave to me
35 As vines going eagerly up; they twine
My life with other leaves, my time
Is hidden in theirs, their thrills are mine.

D. H. LAWRENCE

1 Compose three multiple-choice questions (of four options each) on this poem.

2 Create an original image to express oneness as the poet does in the last four lines.

3 Work out the rhyme scheme of lines 1 to 21.

Choice

I have no wish to travel faster than sound.
I dislike gadgetry and fashion; the mass-cult
of enervating affluence; and I'm sick of the
superfluous, the dull accumulation for
5 accumulation's sake.
Chemical pollutants of environment and diet
are abhorrent to me. Spare me petrol fumes;
bloodless meat; dehydrated sustenance.
Slow down the wheels.
10 Philistinic self-indulgence is no substitute
for life; show me science geared to the
humanities; today's substance instead of
tomorrow's shadow; and what I need for what
I am supposed to want, am badgered to buy.
15 Show me high literacy rates;
low infantile mortality rates;
the life-enhancing quality of simple things.
Spare me the liar and the humbug.

GORDON ALLEN NORTH

────────────

1 Give a specific, concrete example from modern-day life which
represents each of the 'negatives' listed by the poet in this poem.
Do the same thing for the 'positives' he craves.

2 Does this poem remind you of Cecil Gray's poem in Part 2 (p.62)?
Discuss in what way the ideas expressed may be similar.

Anancy

Anancy is a spider;
Anancy is a man;
Anancy's West Indian
And West African.

5   Sometimes, he wears a waistcoat;
Sometimes, he carries a cane;
Sometimes, he sports a top hat;
Sometimes, he's just a plain,
Ordinary, black, hairy spider.

10   Anancy is vastly cunning,
Tremendously greedy,
Excessively charming,
Hopelessly dishonest,
Warmly loving,
15   Firmly confident,
Fiercely wild,
A fabulous character,
Completely out of our mind
And out of his, too.

20   Anancy is a master planner,
A great user
Of other people's plans;
He pockets everybody's food,
Shelter, land, money, and more;
25   He achieves mountains of things,
Like stolen flour dumplings;
He deceives millions of people,
Even the man in the moon;
And he solves all the mysteries
30   On earth, in air, under sea.

And always,
Anancy changes
From a spider into a man
And from a man into a spider
35   And back again
At the drop of a sleepy eyelid.

ANDREW SALKEY

1 Arrange this poem for verse speaking with your class group.

2 Look at verse 3. Write a verse like it using adverbs and adjectives
of your own to describe a colourful character you know.

In our Land

In our land,
Poppies do not spring
From atoms of young blood,
So gaudily where men have died:
5   In our land,
Stiletto cane blades
Sink into our hearts,
And drink our blood.

In our land
10   Sin is not deep,
And bends before the truth,
Asking repentantly for pardon:
In our land,
The ugly stain
15   That blotted Eden garden
Is skin deep only.

In our land,
Storms do not strike
For territory's fences,
20   Elbow room, nor breathing spaces:
In our land,
The hurricane
Of clashes breaks our ranks
For tint of eye.

25   In our land,
We do not breed
That taloned king, the eagle,
Nor make emblazonry of lions:
In our land,
30   The black birds
And the chickens of our mountains
Speak our dreams.

HAROLD M. TELEMAQUE

---

1 Do you agree with the point the poet makes throughout (in the
   context of your own homeland)?

2 Can you give concrete illustrations of the sorts of claims the poet
   makes in stanza two?

3 Write a verse of poetry about your homeland in the same style and
   on the same theme as Telemaque's poem.

88

Ave-Maria

From a church across the street
  Children repeat
Hail Mary, full of Grace;
Skipping the syllables, Follow-the-Leader pace.

5   A little girl (the Lord is with Thee).
    White in organdy,
Lifts her starched, black face
  Towards the barricaded altar
Meadowed in lace.

10 (Blessed art Thou among women.)
    Her child's fingers string the coloured beads
One after one.
(Blessed is the fruit of Thy womb);
Yea, and blessed, too, ripe fruit on trees window-close
15 Under a tropical sun.

Bend low the laden bough
  Child-high; sweeten her incense-flavoured breath
With food, good Mary. (Holy Mary, Mother of God,
20 Pray for us sinners.) And for the blameless —
  Now, before the hour of their death.

                                    BARBARA FERLAND

———————————

1 This poem is presented in a lighthearted and amusing style but
  conveys a serious message. What is that message? Why and how
  has the poet used humour to convey it? Has she succeeded in
  getting her message across effectively?

2 Using another prayer that you know, try to create the same sort of
  effect as the poet has done.

In Memoriam

A nun for all her holiness dies
Like other people
— No tears or flowers at Christmas
And only sometimes remembrance blossoming
5   Amid the rank running weeds of her grave.

I try but cannot write my affection
Nor my gratitude tell
In the swift turned phrase the
Close rhymed syllable you would have loved.

10   — So this my only rosemary
Once more to kneel
Near your nightblack robes
Listening the while
Your voice dreams stories of princes
15   For the lonely boy.

ALFRED PRAGNELL

---

1 Very briefly, what is this poem about? Remember to represent its
content, meaning and tone in your written answer.

2 Prepare two short-answer questions on this poem.

The Tide

Like a piece of driftwood on the shore,
I wait;
Like a seashell cupping unshed tears,
I wait —
5 Till the fisherman counts his catch,
Till the light merges into darkness,
Till the birds are seen no more
And the sea murmurs, now softly,
Now harshly, now softly;

10 And I wait,
With my hands clasped around my knees,
My toes buried in the sand,
My hair blowing in the wind,
My face wet;
15 And I wait,
Asking, Why, why should this be ?

But the sea overwhelms me,
Sweeping away all doubts, all fears,
Making all shrink in humility
20 Before this overpowering immensity;
And I am dwarfed into insignificance,
Like a grain of sand,

Like a piece of driftwood
Left on this desolate shore
25 With the ebbing of the tide,
Alone, unrecognisable
In this vast world
Of sky, of sea, of living creatures.

Like a seashell, now empty,
30 Echoing the murmur of the sea,
Nothing is left now
But a memory,
Nothing is left
But the salt clinging close
35 To my skin.

BEVINDA NORONHA

1 Paint a picture in verse, of yourself waiting somewhere. Start off
   as the poet does in stanza 2: 'And I wait...' Ask a different
   question at the end of the stanza.

2 Compose two multiple-choice questions on the use of simile and
   onomatopoeia in the poem.

The Maroon Girl

I see her on a lonely forest track,
Her level brows made salient by the sheen
Of flesh the hue of cinnamon. The clean
Blood of the hunted, vanished Arawak
5 Flows in her veins with blood of white and black.
Maternal, noble-breasted is her mien;
She is a peasant, yet she is a queen.
She is Jamaica poised against attack.
Her woods are hung with orchids; the still flame
10 Of red hibiscus lights her path, and starred
With orange and coffee blossoms is her yard.
Fabulous, pitted mountains close the frame.
She stands on ground for which her fathers died;
Figure of savage beauty, figure of pride.

WALTER ADOLPHE ROBERTS

1 Work out the rhyme scheme of this poem.

2 Make up a metaphor of your own to fit in with the sentiments of
the poem. Start, 'She is...' Do the same using your own simile.

3 Compose three short-answer questions on the poem to ask your
classmates.

from Isabella

With her two brothers this fair lady dwelt,
    Enriched from ancestral merchandise,
And for them many a weary hand did swelt
    In torched mines and noisy factories,
5 And many once proud-quivered loins did melt
    In blood from stinging whip; − with hollow eyes
Many all day in dazzling river stood,
    To take the rich-ored driftings of the flood.

For them the Ceylon diver held his breath,
10   And went all naked to the hungry shark;
For them his ears gushed blood; for them in death
    The seal on the cold ice with piteous bark
Lay full of darts; for them alone did seethe
    A thousand men in troubles wide and dark:
15 Half-ignorant, they turned an easy wheel,
    That set sharp racks at work, to pinch and peel.

JOHN KEATS

---

1 The above two stanzas are taken from Keats's 'Isabella'. Read and
explore them carefully before attempting the activity that follows.

2 The following is yet another extract from the poem 'Isabella'.
Your job is to rewrite the lines as a stanza with the same pattern
as the two above.

Who hath not loitered in a green church-yard, and let his spirit,
like a demon-mole, work through the clayey-soil and gravel hard,
to see scull, coffin'd bones, and funeral stole; pitying each form
that hungry death hath marred, and filling it once more with
human soul? Ah! this is holiday to what was felt when Isabella by
Lorenzo knelt.

'Is there anybody there?' said the Traveller,
   Knocking on the moonlit door;
And his horse in the silence champed the grasses
   Of the forest's ferny floor:
5   And a bird flew up out of the turret,
   Above the Traveller's head:
And he smote upon the door again a second time;
   'Is there anybody there?' he said.
But no one descended to the Traveller;
10   No head from the leaf-fringed sill
Leaned over and looked into his grey eyes,
   Where he stood perplexed and still.
But only a host of phantom listeners
   That dwelt in the lone house then
15   Stood listening in the quiet of the moonlight
   To that voice from the world of men:
Stood thronging the faint moonbeams on the dark stair,
   That goes down to the empty hall,
Hearkening in an air stirred and shaken
20   By the lonely Traveller's call.
And he felt in his heart their strangeness,
   Their stillness answering his cry,
While his horse moved, cropping the dark turf,
   'Neath the starred and leafy sky;
25   For he suddenly smote on the door, even
   Louder, and lifted his head: —
'Tell them I came, and no one answered,
   That I kept my word', he said.
Never the least stir made the listeners,
30   Though every word he spake
Fell echoing through the shadowiness of the still house
   From the one man left awake:
Ay, they heard his foot upon the stirrup,
   And the sound of iron on stone,
35   And how the silence surged softly backward,
   When the plunging hoofs were gone.

                WALTER DE LA MARE

1 Give a suitable title to the poem, related to any unanswered questions which may persist in your mind after examining the poem fully.

2 Compose three short-answer questions on the poem dealing with mood, figurative language and the silent response from the listeners.

3 Arrange this poem in parts for choral speaking, and try it out with a group.

Do not Go Gentle into
that Good Night

Do not go gentle into that good night,
Old age should burn and rave at close of day;
Rage, rage against the dying of the light.

Though wise men at their end know dark is right,
5 Because their words have forked no lightning they
Do not go gentle into that good night.

Good men, the last wave by, crying how bright
Their frail deeds might have danced in a green bay,
Rage, rage against the dying of the light.

10 Wild men who caught and sang the sun in flight,
and learn, too late, they grieved it on its way,
Do not go gentle into that good night.

Grave men, near death, who see with blinding sight
Blind eyes could blaze like meteors and be gay,
15 Rage, rage against the dying of the light.

And you, my father, there on the sad height,
Curse, bless, me now with your fierce tears, I pray.
Do not go gentle into that good night.
Rage, rage against the dying of the light.

DYLAN THOMAS

---

1 Make up two short-answer questions on the poem.

2 Examine the images in each stanza and comment on them.

3 Imagine it is your father to whom the poet speaks. Write a letter
   to him (your father) persuading him in your own words not to 'go
   gentle into that good night', but 'rage against the dying of the
   light'.

The Pawpaw

Four little boys, tattered,
Fingers and faces splattered
With mud, had climbed
In the rain and caught
5   A pawpaw which they brought,
Like a bomb, to my house. I saw
Then coming: a serious, mumbling,
Tumbling bunch who stopped
At the steps in a hunch.
10   Releasing the fruit from the leaf
It was wrapped in, I watched them
Carefully wash the pawpaw
Like a nugget of gold. This done,
With rainwater, till it shone,
15   They climbed into the house
To present the present to me.
A mocking sign of the doom of all flesh?
Or the purest gold in the kingdom?

EDWARD KAMAU BRATHWAITE

1   Did the poet know the boys or not? Justify your answer.

2   Write a short but detailed paragraph on this poem. Start 'In this
poem . . .' Be sure to include your interpretation of the poet's
ending questions.

Behind Shutters

I knew
I had heard it
somewhere before

he said
his father lived
behind shutters
like
"if once
you let yourself care
the crying
might never stop"

and listening
to the printed word
I looked back
over the years
at a face
absorbing the shock
of the idea
of not liking
to be liked

and knew again
the continuing truth
that
whether you admit or not
to caring
once you let yourself
care
for the abstract
or the live

the crying
might never stop

but then again
the joy
might never end

MERLE COLLINS

1 How does the poet qualify, by extension, the view that one cannot risk caring, even once, for fear of being hurt?

2 On what note does the poem end?

3 Do you know of, or have you heard about someone who would not allow him- or herself to get involved, to love, to give, to care, and to share? If so, relate your story to the class. Perhaps you have known someone who changed this behaviour and 'came out of his shell'. How did that affect his or her life?

Beggarman

That you should come
Crawling
Like a common worm
Into my yard
5   Ragged and odorous
Screwing up your face
In unimaginable agony
And with a gesture ultimate in despair
Stretch out your hand
10 Palm upwards
Begging

Go away, I have nothing.
So much for charity
A barefaced slap
15 Dazed and puzzled he stood
Waiting
Waiting as if that cracked picture of man
Could storm the barricaded conscience
Waiting with walled patience
20 Go away, I repeated fiercely. Nothing.
Surprise wiped patience
Hurt, surprise
Anger, hurt
It was done
25 The unpardonable offence committed
I chased from my doorstep
A beggarman
Hungry

And what of the ultimate insult to manhood
30 Committed by this scarecrow
Why in this vast and vaunted freedomage
Should he
Wearing the rags of his decayed inheritance
Self-pitying, self-humiliating

35 Face furrowed with a thousand years
Of trampling on
Why come to stand before me
A mocking testament
Even my dog begs with more dignity

40 You scarecrow in my yard
Your grotesquerie is a lie
Carved on the conscience of time
That we are brothers
You deny the wasted manhood
45 Coursing your stiff bones
If you want what I have
Earn it
Lie rob burn kill
Assert your right to life
50 Win the shuddering admiration
Of a world grown weary with humility
But do not, do not
Stand there
A broken dumb image of a man
55 Palm upstretched
Accusingly
You'll get no judgment here

So he turned away with his hurt angry look
Ill-masking hate
60 Went out my garden gate like a sick dog
Empty
And in my pocket burned
Three bright red pennies
And in my bones
65 A twisted agony
Go away
I hate you
Brother

ERROL HILL

1 Comment on the use of irony and hyperbole in the poem.

2 Examine the poem and work out how you would arrange it for various voices for choral speaking. Make notes. Compare your arrangement with that of your neighbour.

3 Do you share the poet's views? Give reasons for your answer.

Shoppin' Trips

Sophisticated Nassau gals
Are fin'in' erry day
Dat shoppin' in dey local shops,
Mos' certainly don' pay.

5   De goods dem cheap, de price too dear,
Beside, dey ain' de fad,
But what is worse, too many buy
De same, an' dat is bad.

One time Miami was de place
10   Fa Nassau gals to shop;
But now, too many fine dat out,
An' let da habit drop.

So now, New York is where dey go
Ta furnish out deyself,
15   An' bring back all de lates' style,
Wid not a penny lef'.

Den out ta parties dey will go
Ta show off all dey tings,
Ta prance aroun' an' flutter 'bout
20   Like peacock on de wings.

But as dese swingin' gals step in,
One look gee dem de clue,
Dey hostess had de same idea,
She bin ta New York, too.

SUSAN WALLACE

---

1   Write an additional stanza or two in the same style using the
    dialect of your island. Make your verse tell of the reaction of the
    'swinging gals' to what they discover in the last stanza and
    perhaps what they decide to do.

On a Spaniel Called Beau
Killing a Young Bird

A Spaniel, Beau, that fares like you,
    Well-fed, and at his ease,
Should wiser be, than to pursue
    Each trifle that he sees.

5 But you have kill'd a tiny bird,
    Which flew not till to-day
Against my orders, whom you heard
    Forbidding you the prey.

Nor did you kill, that you might eat,
10   And ease a doggish pain,
For him, though chas'd with furious heat,
    You left where he was slain.

Nor was he of the thievish sort,
    Or one whom blood allures,
15 But innocent was all his sport,
    Whom you have torn for yours.

My dog! what remedy remains
    Since, teach you all I can,
I see you, after all my pains,
20   So much resemble man!

WILLIAM COWPER

---

1 Think of the kind of defence that the spaniel, Beau, might put up
against this complaint, and write a paragraph in which Beau tries
to account for and justify his behaviour.

Moments

Nothing depresses so much as when, caught
Suddenly unawares, the heart and memory

Come face to face and find forgotten pain
In a remembered glance or touch that sought

5   To ease that very hurt. And when, in vain
Later, one tries to fill some emptiness

With some moment that the heart should leave to
Memory, nothing depresses so much.

JOHN ROBERT LEE

1 Have you ever experienced the sort of feelings the poet describes?
Look at the irony expressed in the poem and try to explain it in
your own words.

2 Attempt a poem of four lines starting either as the poet does,
'Nothing depresses so much as...', or 'Nothing delights so
much as...'

The Microbe

The Microbe is so very small
You cannot make him out at all,
But many sanguine people hope
To see him through a microscope.
His jointed tongue that lies beneath
A hundred curious rows of teeth;
His seven tufted tails with lots
Of lovely pink and purple spots,
On each of which a pattern stands,
Composed of forty separate bands;
His eyebrows of a tender green;
All these have never yet been seen —
But Scientists, who ought to know,
Assure us that they must be so...
Oh! let us never, never doubt
What nobody is sure about!

                              HILAIRE BELLOC

1 Write a few lines of prose on whether or not you like this poem,
giving your reasons. How did it make you feel? What reaction did
it elicit from you?

A Carol in Minor

When you have wrapped the last packet,
Sealed the last message, signed
The last wish, tucked
The last forgotten friendship in the envelope;
5   When you have finished trying to bind
This year's sins in pretty little
Confessions of red paper,

Then pause once or twice
Under the gay fragments
10   Of tinsel Christs
That you have hung about you,

And confess yourself
Ready for every man's goodwill...

Does it matter if you fell
15   Bored of your own worshipping
When your rubbled stars could tell
Of no saviour's purchasing
Unto his blood your poverty?

Does it matter if after
20   Two days of love you will sweep
All your broken pints of laughter
Into the last flaccid heap
Of this year's garbage of prosperity?

We are not wise enough for sorrow,
25   And our confessions come
Only to clear a path
For the next sin.

So next year's proffered candy
Will take care of its own atonements,
30   And the tinsel gods will briefly tide
Your quick devotions, and wine
Will be handy to hide
The Christless glare
Of your rubbled star-in-the-east;
35   And you will —
Under new fragments — confess yourself
Ready for every man's goodwill.

E. McG. KEANE

1 Try to pick out some themes in this poem, and relate them to the overall meaning of the poem.

2 Compose two multiple-choice questions (of four options each) on this poem.

from The Torchbearers

His facts fell into place, their broken edges
Joined, like the fragments of a vast mosaic,
And, slowly, the new picture of the world,
Emerging in majestic pageantry
5   Out of the primal dark, before him grew;
Grew by its own inevitable law;
Grew, and earth's ancient fantasies dwindled down;
The stately fabric of the old creation
Crumbled away; while man, proud demi-god
10 Stripped of all arrogance now, priest, beggar, king,
Captive and conqueror, all must own alike
Their ancient lineage. Kin to the dumb beasts
By the red life that flowed through all their veins
From hearts of the same shape, beating all as one
15 In man and brute; kin by those kindred forms
Of flesh and bone, with eyes and ears and mouths
That saw and heard and hungered like his own,
His mother earth reclaimed him. Back and back,
He traced them, till the last faint clue died out
20 In lifeless earth and sea.

ALFRED NOYES

1   The above extract presents a picture of Charles Darwin at his
    home, turning over in his mind all the evidence he has collected
    over the years and coming at last to his great conclusion. Knowing
    this, you should have no difficulty defining the 'new picture of the
    world' that grew before him. What is it?

2   In your own words write a paragraph on the substance of this
    extract. Begin something like this: 'The pieces of scientific
    evidence which Darwin had piled up, began to fit together into
    one large picture.' Now continue.

Spring Feast

When the Roman soldier laughed
And showed his money
I was Magdalene.

When Judas counted coins
With double-entry envy,
Finding no means to appropriate,
I was he.

I was Peter
When he warmed himself
By the burning coals
And looked not at the accusing maid.

I was the darkened sun,
My heart the riven earth.
Now I am the Easter sun arisen,
The wind-tipped eagle
Scalloping across the sky.

Magdalene I was,
Judas, Peter;
Now I am the risen Lord.

JOHN FIGUEROA

1 Think of a negative and unfortunate situation in which you found
yourself and from which you emerged whole, enlightened and a
better person. Write some lines in the spirit of stanza 4 expressing
your experience and registering the change of mood in the present
you. Use metaphorical lines all the way.

Pygmalion and Galatea

Alas, now I look back I think
He loved me in his way,
But his fingers had the potter's itch
To model angels out of clay.

5　He tried to put me on a pedestal
And keep me there for all the world to see
While all I asked for was his heart, a hearth, a home —
Small comfort and some privacy.

Oh I was not built for worship but for love —
10　I who wanted warmth and gaiety
The shouts of children on the sandy beach —
Must needs endure this cold solemnity,
Receive the votive gifts, the sacrifical dove,
Bestow the charming smile, the appropriate speech,
15　And make a monument of love.

Oh, the weight of such devotion was too much for me to bear
Nor could I stand the curious look
The studied courteous regard
Men throw upon another's idol . . .

20　And I, no princess from a story book,
Small wonder that I fled his patient care,
For empty worship is its own reward
And I a creature made of flesh and blood — not marble.

H. D. CARBERRY

1　Discuss the relevance of the title. If you do not know the
legend to which it refers, do some research on it for the next
class.

2　Compose two multiple-choice questions (of four options each) on
this poem.

3　Now compose two short-answer questions also.

I Shall Go Back

I shall go back yes, I shall
To stroll and laugh again along the avenues
Watch the golden sunset unfold
Its flaming light through the mango trees.
I shall go back to wander by the garden lawns,
And admire once more the Victoria Lily pond
Watch the Manatee come to feed when called.
Dreams of yesterday that seem so very long.
I shall go back to hear distant Indian drums
Calling the guest to the marriage feast.
Indian songs of native life love and peace
Intoxicating hidden thoughts so deep.
I shall go back again yes, I shall
To quiet this longing which in my heart abides.

WILMOT SANOWAR

1 Go back to 'Flame-heart' by Claude McKay on page 68. Compare
  and contrast it with this poem. Look at similarities and
  differences.

2 In order to remind yourself of the intention of each of the poems
  in Part III, look back at them and make a short statement on
  each, demonstrating its aim and purpose.

Tempus

Time can tighten its tentacles
or
loosen its chains
Can free a soul
5   or
Imprison a heart
Time — the snail
and
Time — the jaguar
10   Time the messenger
of peace, of war

Time is
hoping and
loving and
15   seeing and
fearing

Time is
learning
and finding
20   and giving
and telling

Time's changing
Time's remembering
Time's deceiving
25   Time's forgetting

Time is you
Time is me
Time together
not forever

30   TIME IS NOW!

N.R. CARASCO BAILEY

1 Time is such an important and indispensable facet of living. It
enters into all that we are and do. Go back and quickly remind
yourself of each of the poems you have dealt with in this book.
See which aspect or quality of Time is relevant to each. What
does Time mean to *you*? Write down your thoughts, keeping a
simple style but maintaining some rhythm in your phrasing.

2 Which poem in this anthology did you like best? Examine your
feelings about the poem you choose, stating them clearly.

GLOSSARY

Alliteration   The repetition of speech sounds in a sequence of adjacent words. Usually applied to beginning consonants, e.g., 'In the summer season when soft was the sun.'

Antithesis   A contrast or opposition in the meaning of contiguous phrases or clauses, e.g., 'marriage has many pains, but celibacy has no pleasures.'

Blank verse   Non-rhyming verse (with *rhythm* of five pairs of stressed and unstressed syllables). The form of verse closest to the natural rhythm of spoken English, e.g., the extract from Ulysses.

Climax   A building-up of ideas to the highest point, e.g., 'Idler! Thief! Murderer!'

Dialect   The variety of language spoken by a person or group of people from a particular area. See 'Shoppin' Trips', or 'The Muse's Complaint'.

Figurative language   Language used to imply a meaning other than the literal meaning, not to be read for its surface value alone, e.g., *metaphor*, *simile* or *personification*.

Form   The structure, shape and arrangement of a poem, e.g., the sonnet form has 14 lines, which should only follow traditional rhyming patterns.

Free verse   Short lines of irregular length, lacking *rhyme*. See 'Song of Myself.'

Hyperbole   Exaggeration for the sake of effect, e.g., 'I've lived through thousands of New Year celebrations.'

Imagery   All the objects and qualities in a poem that strike our senses (whether *figurative* or *literal*).

Irony   A phrase or statement intended to convey the opposite of its *literal* meaning, e.g., 'How nice of you to be late today for a change.' Irony is also being used when the appearance contradicts the true situation and what the reader or the individual in the poem expects to happen is not what occurs.

Literal language   Language intended to be taken at face value, conveying exactly what it says, as it might be in normal speech.

Litotes   Understatement for effect, often *ironic*; the opposite of *hyperbole*, e.g. 'He is no fool.'

Metaphor   The application of a quality or action to something to which it is not applicable in *literal* terms, e.g., 'The king is an ass.'

Mood   See Note to the Reader.

Onomatopoeia   The use of words which seem to sound like the noises or things they represent, e.g., hiss, tap, buzz, plop, zip.

Oxymoron   Where an utterance contains two terms that in ordinary usage are opposites, e.g., 'pleasing pains', 'terrible beauty'.

Paradox   A statement which appears to be self-contradictory or absurd, yet makes good sense, e.g., 'the greater the truth, the greater the libel.'

Personification   Where an inanimate object or an abstract concept is described in human terms, e.g., 'Sky lowered, and muttering thunder, some sad drops wept.'

Rhetorical question   One asked to confirm hearer's attention rather than to elicit reply, e.g., 'O Wind, if Winter comes, can Spring be far behind?', i.e., questioner already knows the answer.

Rhyme   Words of similar sounds used in similar positions at the ends of two following or alternate lines, or within a line.

Rhythm   A recognisable, though variable, pattern in the beat of the stresses in the stream of sound.

Run-on line   Where the sense of one line of verse runs over directly into that of the next needing no pause between verse lines.

Satire   The art of projecting a serious message by making it seem ridiculous, evoking attitudes of amusement, contempt, or scorn in order to make it memorable or create the required effect.

Simile   The description of one thing by comparison with another, using the words 'like' or 'as', e.g., 'as red as blood'.

Stanza   A grouping of lines in a poem, set off by a space in the printed text.

Symbolism   The use of a word or phrase which represents some greater thing beyond itself, some larger idea, e.g., 'the cross' – sacrifice, resurrection, salvation, etc., 'the dove' – peace, 'total darkness' – death.

Tone   See Note to the Reader.

Turning point   A noticeable change occurring in the poem: of time, mood, tone, scene, situation or idea, for example.

INDEX OF POETS
AND POEMS

Armstrong, Martin, *England*
Mrs Reece Laughs   18
Auden, W.H., *England*
Underneath the Abject Willow   14
Barrow, Raymond, *Belize*
Dawn is a Fisherman   2
Bell, Vera, *Jamaica*
Ancestor on the Auction Block   60
Belloc, Hilaire, *England*
The Microbe   105
Brathwaite, Edward Kamau, *Barbados*
The Pawpaw   97
Browning, Robert, *England*
The grey sea   12
Campbell, George, *Jamaica*
History Makers   78
Carasco Bailey, N.R., *St Lucia*
Tempus   112
Carberry, H.D., *Jamaica*
Pygmalion and Galatea   110
Carter, Martin, *Guyana*
Looking at your Hands   82
Castillo, Otto Rene, *Guatemala*
Before the Scales, Tomorrow   65
Collymore, Frank, *Barbados*
Homage to Planters   6
Collins, Merle, *Grenada*
Behind Shutters   98
Cowper, William, *England*
On a Spaniel Called Beau Killing
a Young Bird   103
Craig, Dennis, *Guyana*
Flowers   43
Cunningham, James Vincent, *England*
The Fox and the Cat   56
de la Mare, Walter, *England*
The Listeners   94
Dickinson, Emily, *U.S.A.*
Like rain it sounded   22
Diop, David, *Senegal*
Africa my Africa   20
Ellis, Royston, *Dominica*
In the Gentle Afternoon   51
Ferland, Barbara, *Jamaica*
Ave Maria   89
Figueroa, John, *Jamaica*
Spring Feast   109

Forde, A.N., *Barbados*
Canes by the Roadside   52
Goldsmith, Oliver, *England*
In all my wanderings   4
Gray, Cecil, *Trinidad and Tobago*
A Wheel Called Progress   62
Hendriks, A.L., *Jamaica*
Road to Lacovia   50
Hill, Errol, *Trinidad and Tobago*
Beggarman   100
Hippolyte, Kendel, *St Lucia*
The Muse's Complaint   54
Hughes, Ted, *England*
Hawk Roosting   64
Keane, E. McG., *St Vincent*
A Carol in Minor   106
Keats, John, *England*
Isabella   93
Lamb, Mary, *England*
Feigned Courage   26
Lawrence, D.H., *England*
The Best of School   84
Lee, John Robert, *St Lucia*
Moments   104
Leigh, H.S., *England*
'Twas Ever Thus   70
Lucie-Smith, Edward, *Jamaica*
The Lesson   45
Mais, Roger, *Jamaica*
Light Love   66
Marson, Una, *Jamaica*
Where Death Was Kind   36
McFarlane, Basil, *Jamaica*
Music a Kind of Sleep   79
McKay, Claude, *Jamaica*
Flame-heart   68
Miles, Judy, *Trinidad and Tobago*
Lunch Hour   46
Morris, Mervyn, *Jamaica*
Little Boy Crying   24
Nash, Ogden, *U.S.A.*
A Solution   42
Noronha, Bevinda, *Kenya*
The Tide   91
North, Gordon Allen, *England*
Choice   86

Noyes, Alfred, *U.S.A.*
  The Torchbearers 108
Owen, Wilfred, *England*
  The Send-off 58
Pragnell, Alfred, *Barbados*
  In Memoriam 90
Ramon-Fortuné, Barnabas J.,
    Trinidad and Tobago
  The Riders 71
Reeves, James, *England*
  Academic 41
Roberts, Sally, *West Indies*
  A Small Tragedy 77
Roberts, Walter Adolphe, *Jamaica*
  The Maroon Girl 92
Roethke, Theodore, *U.S.A.*
  Elegy 8
Salkey, Andrew, *Jamaica*
  Anancy 87
Sanowar, Wilmot, *Trinidad and
    Tobago*
  I Shall Go Back 111
Scott, Dennis, *Jamaica*
  Bird 48
Seymour, A.J., *Guyana*
  Carrion Crows 76
Shakespeare, William, *England*
  Sonnet 44
Sherlock, Sir Philip, *Jamaica*
  Jamaican Fisherman 40

Shirley, James, *England*
  Death the Leveller 10
Telemaque, Harold M., *Trinidad and
    Tobago*
  In our Land 88
Tennyson, Alfred, Lord, *England*
  Ulysses 72
Thomas, Dylan, *Wales*
  Do not Go Gentle into that Good
  Night 96
Thumboo, Edwin, *Singapore*
  Ahmad 28
Treece, Henry, *England*
  Conquerors 30
Vaughan, H.A., *Barbados*
  Revelation 34
Walcott, Derek, *St Lucia*
  Elegy 16
Wallace, Susan, *Bahamas*
  Shoppin' Trips 102
Whitman, Walt, *U.S.A.*
  Song of Myself 80
Wordsworth, William, *England*
  Upon Westminster Bridge 32
Wotton, Sir Henry, *England*
  Character of a Happy Life 83